"*Co-parenting 101* c_____nation, and tool for parents that ca_____ well as a tremendous amoun_____ this boo. not only to _____ ult when difficult sit_____ mplating

"As a marital and couples therapist, I have witnessed how contentious divorces affect both the parents and their children. It can be agonizing. I would highly recommend and encourage those folks contemplating divorce to read this book first. It is extremely practical with many vignettes of actual parent struggles, including the authors' own co-parenting journey. The interview with the authors' daughter is particularly touching and poignant, a powerful message for all divorced parents."

—**Bari Benjamin, LCSW, BCD**, licensed, clinical
    social worker

"An extraordinary book and required reading for separated and divorced parents, as well as mental health practitioners. [*Co-parenting 101*] outlines some of the possible pitfalls of the co-parenting process with which clinicians like myself are all too familiar and regularly deal with therapeutically. But now we can refer parents to *Co-parenting 101* to help them mindfully approach the co-parenting process and examine the array of options they have in their parenting toolbox."

—**Robert F. Fierstein, PhD**, licensed ___

"Deesha Philyaw and Michael D. Thomas have done the impossible. This formerly married couple not only co-parent their children without rancor, but in *Co-parenting 101*, they teach us how to do it, too. What a helpful, detailed, and realistic guide to a widespread but much ignored situation! This book will help readers navigate the tricky and often treacherous waters of co-parenting with a former partner."

—**Ericka Lutz**, author of *The Complete Idiot's Guide to Stepparenting*

"As a family physician, I care for hundreds of families with parents living separately. The mental and physical health of children is directly impacted by the relationship between their co-parents. I'm recommending this book to every separated family I see. If parents were willing to step up and consider the suggestions made in *Co-parenting 101*, their kids would be healthier and far more resilient!"

—**Deborah Gilboa, MD**, of askdoctorg.com

Co-parenting
101

Helping Your
Kids Thrive in
Two Households
after Divorce

Deesha Philyaw
Michael D. Thomas

New Harbinger Publications, Inc.

Publisher's Note

Distributed in Canada by Raincoast Books

Copyright © 2013 by Deesha Philyaw and Michael D. Thomas
New Harbinger Publications, Inc.
5674 Shattuck Avenue
Oakland, CA 94609
www.newharbinger.com

Acquired by Melissa Kirk; Cover design by Amy Shoup; Edited by Will DeRooy; Text design by Tracy Carlson

Library of Congress Cataloging-in-Publication Data

Philyaw, Deesha.
  Co-parenting 101 : helping your kids thrive in two households after divorce / Deesha Philyaw and Michael D. Thomas.
    pages cm
  Includes bibliographical references.
  ISBN 978-1-60882-463-2 (pbk. : alk. paper) -- ISBN 978-1-60882-464-9 (pdf e-book) -- ISBN 978-1-60882-465-6 (epub) 1. Children of divorced parents. 2. Parenting, Part-time. 3. Divorced parents. 4. Joint custody of children. I. Thomas, Michael D., 1971- II. Title. III. Title: Co-parenting one hundred one. IV. Title: Co-parenting one hundred and one.
  HQ777.5.P48 2013
  306.89--dc23
                              2013003020

Printed in the United States of America

15 14 13   10 9 8 7 6 5 4 3 2

To Taylor, Peyton, Troi, Lauren, and CEF with love

—D.P.

To C., Taylor, Peyton, and Mika. You are both
the "how" and the "why" in my co-parenting
journey. I love you!

—M.D.T.

Contents

Part III
"But You Don't Know *My* Ex"

Acknowledgments

Many people supported this book before it was a book at all. We thank Wednesday Martin, PhD; Robert F. Fierstein, PhD; Tony Norman; Cora Daniels; Yvonne Kelly of the Step and Blended Family Institute; Troy Johnson of the African American Literature Book Club; parenting coordinator Brooke Randolph for wise, wise counsel; Chris Ivey and Rebecca Cech for their love and manual labor; Kenneth Crudup for his brilliance; Laura Szabo-Cohen for providing sustenance; Ericka Lutz for her first-reader keen eye; Kim Ellis (aka Dr. Goddess) for her tireless cheerleading on our behalf and on behalf of children and families; Catherine Greeno and Andi Fischhoff for their "on the ground" support of us and our blog *Co-Parenting 101*; and Talibah Mbonisi for pretty much everything. For innumerable acts of kindness and help, we also appreciate Jennifer James Soto, Lissett Oliveri; Andrea Morgan; Taneshia Nash Laird; Heather Hetchler; Kim Daboo; Faith Adiele; Genie Maples; Tami Winfrey Harris; Carolyn Edgar; Yona Harvey; members of the CoParenting101.org Facebook group; and all our Twitter followers. Special thanks to the Flight School crew (Joe Dziekan, Jasdeep Khaira, and Courtney Ehrlichman), literary agent extraordinaire Danielle Chiotti; and Will DeRooy and the smart, keen-eyed folks at New Harbinger Publications. To everyone else who has graciously helped make this book possible, please charge the omission of your names to our faulty memories and not to our hearts.

Introduction: "You Should Write a Book"

In the spring of 2005, we delivered some news to our then-six-year-old daughter Taylor that broke her heart. We told her that we were divorcing because we had grown-up problems we could not fix, even though we'd tried very, very hard. We explained what divorce meant: the two of us would live in separate houses, and she and her eighteen-month-old sister, Peyton, would stay with each of us on different days. We told Taylor all of the ways our lives would change because of the divorce, and we told her all of the things that would remain the same—especially our love for and commitment to her and Peyton. She still had a family, we reassured her.

Taylor's reaction was one that is common to many children of divorce. "I made up a word for what I feel," she told us a few days after our initial conversation. "I'm *smad*. Sad and mad at the same time." We knew that we couldn't take away her hurt entirely, but we made a pact to avoid compounding the pain and upheaval in our children's lives. Through the sometimes tense legal process and the awkward early days of negotiating the day-to-day details of parenting across two households, we put aside our own wounds and concentrated on the most important task at hand: making sure we acted in our children's best interest, emotionally and practically.

After our marriage ended, we became the poster children for divorce in our circle of friends and colleagues. We wish we could have been the poster children for successful marriage, but it didn't work out that way.

Instead, we have managed to establish a congenial co-parenting relationship that allows our children to thrive and that causes those who know us to ask, "How in the world do you do it?" There are simple and not-so-simple answers to that question—answers we have shared with other divorced couples, those contemplating divorce, and adult children of divorce through our blog *Co-Parenting 101* and online radio show *CoParenting Matters*. Inevitably, the response we get is "You should write a book." So we did.

We are not, however, advocates for divorce. In fact, we tell couples who seek our advice to consider divorce only as their very last option. We won't debate whether staying together "for the sake of the kids" is best for children. That's a personal decision each thoughtful couple must make for themselves. But we've heard from co-parents who say that using "for the sake of the kids" as the glue to hold their troubled marriage together ultimately didn't work. This book is a resource for those parenting after divorce or separation, no matter what the reason for the split.

As divorced co-parents, the question we get most often after "How do you do it?" is "If you can get along this well—well enough to collaborate on this book—why couldn't you make your marriage work?" Our answer: the platonic relationship we've cultivated since our divorce is possible only because we've removed ourselves from the parasitic resentments that ate away at our marriage, from the daily misery and conflict. In other words, we are able to get along now because we are free to have a relationship that is limited to what we *are* good at together: parenting. While co-parenting still forces us to bump up against those raw areas that contributed to the demise of our marriage, we deal with them in a different context now: It's not about us anymore. Our obligations are to our children, and our love for them motivates us to proceed with caution through the rough spots.

We're not alone in pursuing this particular postdivorce path. Through our blog, we've connected with other former couples who tell us that, despite a rocky start, they are doing what at first seemed impossible: striving for civility, compromise, and cooperation. And their children are better off for it.

With straight talk, practical advice, and a dose of humor thrown in for good measure, this book is a guide to help exes become successful co-parents...truly for the sake of the kids.

Once the legal dust settles, children may be the only reason former spouses remain in contact with each other. Every interaction can stoke residual feelings of betrayal, desire for revenge, anger, and disappointment. Those are all typical, understandable post-breakup sentiments, but they do not give anyone a "Get Out of Parenting Free" card, nor do they render either parent expendable in a child's life.

In fact, we believe good parenting after divorce *means* cooperative co-parenting. This book is based on the premise that cooperative co-parenting after a breakup between fit parents is a must, not an option. It is as essential to your child's emotional well-being as nutritious food is to his physical well-being. Research (Kuhn and Guidubaldi 1997; Joakimidis 1994; Bauserman 2002; Center for Parental Responsibility 2004; Shackelton 2006), anecdotal evidence, and plain old common sense bear this out:

- Children benefit from having both of their fit and willing parents play an active role in their lives and from spending substantial time with both parents. (This is the cornerstone of co-parenting.)

- Children look to their parents for reassurance during the difficult time after a breakup. Having both parents involved in their lives—working together to meet their needs—provides more security and stability for children after a breakup.

- Parents who refrain from doing things that put their children in the middle of their conflicts—asking the children to relay messages, denigrating the other parent in front of the children, or forbidding mention of the other parent in their presence—free their children from the stress of loyalty conflicts.

- Co-parented children feel less rejected by their parents, and they report feeling attached to both parents.

- Parents who share custody experience less emotional loss, depression, grief, and anger after a breakup. Happier, healthier parents raise happier, healthier kids.

- On average, children with two actively involved parents fare better in studies of rates of teen pregnancy, suicide, drug abuse, poor academic performance, school dropout, and delinquency.

- Ongoing conflict between parents after divorce increases children's risk factors for depression, behavioral problems, teen pregnancy, suicide, delinquency, and school failure and dropout.

- Co-parenting avoids the false "winner/loser" dichotomy of divorce, casting neither parent as a "visitor" or secondary parent, thus allowing the *child*, ultimately, to win.

Further, as more family courts move away from the traditional mode of thinking about divorce—Mom automatically gets primary custody of the kids, while Dad gets visitation, typically on weekends— mandatory shared custody arrangements are becoming the norm (except in extenuating circumstances, such as proven abuse, neglect, domestic violence, or mental illness that renders one parent unfit). Perhaps you have been given such a mandate as part of your divorce proceedings. This book can equip you and your parenting partner to honor the court-ordered agreement and care for your children together without high levels of conflict.

There are legal and financial benefits to co-parenting as well. Co-parenting significantly reduces child support default (US Bureau of the Census 2011), and co-parents are half as likely to go to back to court to settle their disputes as those without joint custody or visitation arrangements (Joakimidis 1994). Less time stressed out about legal wrangling means more time to be fully present and engaged with your children.

In the wake of divorce, children need to see their parents functioning cooperatively. We know from our own family's experience that to move forward in this way is a challenge, but not an insurmountable one. In the following chapters, we'll offer a blueprint for you to:

+ Establish a new, "working" relationship with your former spouse or partner, one that moves beyond your rocky marital past and looks forward to a more peaceful parenting partnership.

+ Identify specific strategies for co-managing the day-to-day demands of your children's lives, such as schooling, scheduling, health, holidays, and extracurricular activities, across households.

+ Play a positive, meaningful role in your child's life even if your co-parent isn't willing to cooperate.

+ Talk with your child in age-appropriate ways about the breakup, and address her questions and concerns.

+ Understand the different needs of infants, toddlers, school-age children, and teens during a breakup.

+ Address the challenges unique to co-parenting an only child or those unique to co-parenting siblings.

Although shared parenting is in the best interest of most children (Center for Parental Responsibility 2004), we recognize that cooperative co-parenting is not possible if one or both parents refuse to facilitate it. See part III, "But You Don't Know *My* Ex," and remember that your children are worth your best effort regardless of what the other parent does or does not do. That said, co-parenting should never put a child or parent in harm's way.

Okay, So ... What Is Co-parenting, Exactly?

Regardless of the specifics of your physical custody arrangement and parenting time schedule, successful co-parenting can be defined as any postdivorce or post-separation parenting arrangement that (1) fosters continued, healthy relationships for children with *both* parents and (2) is founded on a genuinely cooperative relationship between the parents. "Co-parenting" is often used interchangeably with "joint parenting," "joint custody," "shared custody," and "shared parenting." For a variety of practical reasons, one parent's house may be defined as your child's primary residence, but if every effort is made for her to maintain a close, loving relationship with both parents, then you are a successful co-parent.

Now, we know what you may be thinking: *That whole cooperative co-parenting thing sounds great...in theory. But he cheated on me!* or *But I hate her! Why do you think we're getting a divorce in the first place?* However, putting your kids first requires you to love your child more than you hate your ex. If you're like most parents, you love your children so much that you say you would die for them. But the question is: Will you *live* for them? Will you love them enough to put their need for cooperative co-parenting above the need you may feel to rail against or punish your ex?

While parents may remain mired in the muck that contributed to the end of their relationship, the children are concerned with what the breakup means for *them*. They wonder, "Will I still get to be with Mom *and* Dad? Can I still love them both?" Divorce ends marriages, but families endure. Kids want reassurance that even though the family they have known is breaking up, they are still part of a family in which they receive love and care from both parents, unconditionally.

Cooperative co-parenting after a breakup helps not only your children, but you as well. Minimal conflict between you and your co-parent reduces the stress in your life and allows a mutually beneficial partnership to flourish; you both have someone with whom to share the parenting load. Further, less time and energy spent fighting a cold war (or worse) with your ex gives you more time to enjoy your kids as an engaged, positive, responsive parent.

Perfection Is Not the Goal

Maybe you're still rolling your eyes and thinking *Yeah, right*. And we can't say we blame you. Divorce in American culture is synonymous with combat, not cooperation. Everyone has heard (or suffered through) the horror story of a bitter divorce. But there are other stories, like the story of our own family. You don't often hear these "feel-good" stories because if the post-breakup situation is a peaceful one, presumably there's no story to tell.

We founded the blog *Co-Parenting 101* for precisely this reason: to provide a place for cooperative co-parents to share their stories so that others might be encouraged, and to challenge the stereotype of the always-messy divorce.

Our co-parenting relationship isn't always easy. We've made—and still make—mistakes along the way. The goal is not perfection, but rather an ongoing, sincere effort to cooperate with each other where our children are concerned. We believe that more divorced couples can co-parent successfully if they make a firm commitment to really live for their kids—including honoring and encouraging their kids' relationship with the other parent and seeing that parent as an ally instead of an enemy.

Putting the Kids First

Co-parents should seek to act in the best interest of their children—children who did not ask to be born, who should never be asked to agree that divorce was the right decision, and whose needs should be their parents' primary concern. While it's impossible to meet all of your child's needs all the time—after all, your child would likely say that he *needs* for the two of you to get back together—you'll never hit a target if you don't at least aim for it. If you aim to put your kids' needs first, you're guaranteed more close hits than if you didn't aim at all. Putting the kids first is the foundation for a successful co-parenting relationship—a relationship built for the sake of your children, in spite of the animosity, hurt, and baggage between you and your ex.

Now, when we preach the gospel of Putting the Kids First, we are not minimizing parents' needs, the very real emotions parents wrangle with post-breakup, or the marital history that preceded the breakup. Believe us, we've been there. We know it's not easy, and we hope the strategies offered in this book will help you succeed as a co-parent. But nothing we suggest here, nothing the court orders, and nothing mental health professionals advise will matter unless you embrace the following truth—and we mean this in the nicest possible way:

It's not about you.

Given that you're a parent, this is probably not an earth-shattering revelation. Kids routinely move parents out of their comfort zones. This is as true after your divorce or separation as it was before. Even when she was in utero, your child's needs mattered to you. She became the center of your universe and the topic of nearly every conversation. Children challenge, inconvenience, and push their parents to their limits. Parents change their lifestyles and their priorities for the sake of their children. If need be, parents sacrifice and do without, so that their children may have. The freedom and indulgences they enjoyed before they had children are eroded by kids' never-ending need for time, attention, and basic care and feeding. Every day, in ways large and small, parents put their children's needs before their own grown-up wants.

We aren't suggesting that parents become martyrs, sacrificing all their needs on the altar of Putting the Kids First. For example, successful co-parenting does not require you to be a doormat or to "play nice" and ignore the fact that your ex-husband never calls to say he's going to be late picking up the kids or the fact that your ex-girlfriend is verbally abusive toward you and your new wife. Successful co-parenting requires that you address the discourteous behavior with your ex...when the kids aren't around. It requires that you comfort your disappointed children and acknowledge their feelings... without calling the other parent a selfish jerk, for example. Hugs and affirming words comfort your children. "Your dad is a selfish jerk" comforts no one but you.

But remember: *it's not about you.*

Honoring Your Child's Relationship with Your Ex

Even if *your child* is the one who calls your ex a selfish jerk, remember that this same child still loves that selfish jerk tremendously. The relationship between your ex and your child, however rocky, is sacred. Honor it. Your child is depending on both of you to set aside parental hurts and axes to grind, at least enough to put her needs first. This may require some healing on your part as a prerequisite. If so, skip ahead to chapter 2, "Good Grief: Strategies for Starting the Healing Process."

Now, you might be shaking your head as you read this, thinking: *I'm all for putting the kids first. But you don't know my ex! She's a real basket case. It's been years since the divorce, and she still hates me. Worse, she's trying to turn the kids against me! She'll never go for this co-parenting thing.*

Actually we do know your ex—and countless mothers and fathers just like her. She was married to friends and colleagues of ours and to some of the thousand-plus co-parents who visit our website (coparenting101.org) each month. We may not know your ex personally, but we are quite familiar with the bitterness that needlessly turns children into the collateral damage of divorce. And you're right: your ex may not go for this co-parenting thing, but we encourage you to skip ahead to part III, "But You Don't Know *My* Ex," for some tips on how to be the best co-parent you can be in the face of her resistance.

Parenting after divorce—without all the drama—really is possible. We are living proof. This book contains our ideas and experiences—what's worked for us and what hasn't—as well as what we've learned from other parents (all names of co-parents and their children are pseudonyms). Often in the following chapters, we will use the term "divorce," but we address some of the unique needs of never-married co-parenting families in chapter 10, "What about Us?"

We also presume shared parenting within the same state, but chapters 7, 8, and 10 offer specific information and strategies for non-custodial parents and those who are co-parenting across state lines. Throughout the book, we'll also provide tips for building a strong parenting partnership with a noncustodial or nonresidential parent.

It's our hope that you and your co-parent will craft from these pages a plan that accommodates your personalities and circumstances and, most important, meets the unique needs of your children.

We wish you and your family a successful co-parenting journey!

Part I

Divorce 101

This section will help you lay the groundwork for successful co-parenting. How you mind the details—and your manners—at the outset of your separation and subsequent divorce will influence your children's emotional adjustment and will set the stage for the success—or failure—of your co-parenting relationship. This section will also guide you toward healthy means of coping with your own grief associated with the breakup so that you can help your children heal and adjust as well. Even if you're already divorced or well into the process, read on! This section can affirm your best co-parenting practices or, alternatively, help identify those areas in need of damage control or a co-parenting "do over." It's never too late to act in the best interest of your children.

Chapter 1

Before You Call a Lawyer: Laying the Groundwork for Co-parenting Success

The first commitment I made was that I would be there for the kids physically and financially, no matter what. Before divorce, I shared the parenting responsibility, and I was determined to not be an every-other-weekend parent.

—Carlton, dad of two

Divorce with kids in the mix is a time of intense personal sacrifice, calling for tremendous amounts of maturity and patience—at precisely a time when you're least able to muster them, because it's also a time of tremendous loss and grief. Those who know us from our blog or online radio show often assume that, because we're friendly with each other now, our divorce process was amicable from start to finish. It wasn't. We hurt. We grieved. Threats were made. The f-bomb was dropped. Angry e-mails were fired off at one in the morning. We disagreed about many issues, and loudly.

But one matter on which we were in full agreement from the outset was that we wanted to spare our children as much as possible. We didn't delude ourselves into thinking that divorce wouldn't hurt them, but we did agree to do everything we could not to compound the hurt. We knew it would be easier for our kids if we agreed to do the following:

1.   Never bad-mouth each other to or in earshot of the kids.

2.   Be civil during drop-offs and pick-ups, so that those times of transition would not be laden with our conflict.

3.   Go on occasional whole-family outings, during which the children could spend time with both of us together.

Of these commitments, we believe numbers 1 and 2 are essential to any post-breakup parenting partnership that allows children to heal and ultimately thrive. Number 3 might not appeal to some co-parents, and it's not advisable for those in high-conflict co-parenting situations.

Despite the conflicts that led to the demise of our marriage, and the conflict inherent in separating and divorcing, we still respected each other as parents. This made commitments 1 and 2 pretty easy. Number 3, however, made for some inwardly awkward and uncomfortable moments for us early on. Our kids, however, seemed none the wiser; they loved when we all went out to dinner or for ice cream. They've both shared with us that one of the hardest parts of the divorce is being with one of us *or* the other, so these outings were (and continue to be) cherished times.

These are the commitments we made for our children before either of us picked up the phone and called a lawyer. They formed the basis for our co-parenting ground rules, the foundation upon which we began to build our post-breakup parenting partnership. However, co-parenting is not a one-size-fits-all proposition. Each family's co-parenting ground rules will reflect that family's particular circumstances. Even if your divorce is already final, it's never too late to commit to improving your co-parenting situation.

Establishing Your Ground Rules

Consider the following questions when setting your own co-parenting ground rules. Discuss them explicitly with your child's other parent. If a sit-down conversation isn't feasible, ease into the conversation via e-mail. Or, make these commitments on your own until you are able to have a civil conversation with your ex.

1. Can you both agree to never bad-mouth each other to or in earshot of your kids?

2. Can you both agree to be civil during drop-offs and pick-ups?

3. What other commitments can you both make to your children right now to help them transition and adjust?

4. What are you willing to sacrifice to make the transition and adjustment as easy as possible for your children?

5. Think of your children's unique personalities and needs. What are some specific areas in which they would benefit from your cooperation and civility? For example, if your child plays soccer, commit to attending his games and practices as you normally would, keeping your focus on him and not each other.

After setting some basic ground rules, as you move into the process of separation and divorce, you'll need to make some additional commitments as co-parents.

Commitments for Building a Strong Post-breakup Parenting Partnership

Though raw emotions are running high for both of you (to say the least), for your children's sake, you'll need to sit down with your soon-to-be-ex and talk about how you can work together to minimize the upheaval and conflict your children will experience during the divorce process and beyond. You can commit to strengthening your parenting partnership at any time, even if you're already divorced. And as with the ground rules, you'll want to choose a time to meet when you are both open and calm, or bring up one or two of the following commitments in an e-mail. Or, make these commitments on your own until you are able to communicate with your ex about them.

Commit to putting love for your children and concern for their well-being ahead of your grown-up grievances. In common parlance: love your child more than you hate your ex. Now more than ever, your kids need their parents to provide unconditional love, security, and as much stability and peace as possible, given the circumstances. Consider whether your actions, in the legal process and in daily life, align with who you are as caring, committed parents.

One way to keep your children's welfare at the center of things—without putting them in the middle—is to honor the "Bill of Rights for Children in Divorce and Dissolution Actions," a helpful list of rights that children have in any divorce. Created by the New Jersey Chapter of the Association of Family and Conciliation Courts (DeVaris et al. n.d.), these rights include:

- The right to be treated as important and separate human beings with unique feelings, needs, ideas, and desires, not existing solely to gratify the needs of their parents

- The right to not participate in the painful games parents play to hurt each other or be put in the middle of their battles

+ The right not to be a go-between or a message carrier for their parents

+ The right to a continuing, relaxed, and secure relationship with both parents

+ The right to express love and affection for, and receive love and affection from, both parents

+ The right to know that expressions of love between children and parents will not cause fear, disapproval, or other negative consequences

+ The right to continuing care and guidance from both parents

+ The right to be protected from hearing degrading or bad comments about either parent

+ The right to experience regular, consistent, and flexible shared parenting time with both parents, and the right to know the reason for changes in the parenting schedule

+ The right to not be forced to choose one parent over the other

We'll explore these and other rights in later chapters; the complete "Bill of Rights" can be found at afcc-nj.org/bill_of_rights.html.

Commit to upholding these rights for your kids as you go through divorce proceedings or navigate the aftermath of divorce.

Agree on as many logistical details of co-parenting as possible. On what days and evenings will your child be with each of you? What schedule will allow your child to spend as much time as possible with both parents? This is a practical matter as well as a core concern for your child. How will you handle expenses related to your child's care and decisions regarding health- and education-related issues until a formal agreement is reached? How will you handle this once you are divorced and parenting across two households? See chapter 7 for a detailed discussion of these considerations. Determine how many of these co-parenting basics you can agree upon, and put them in writing, if possible.

At this point in the process of our own separation, we weren't explicit about cooperation with regard to practical matters such as doctors' appointments, buying clothes, and the parenting time schedule. It just seemed to follow that if we were committed to giving the kids our post-breakup best, we'd do whatever we had to in order to make life as simple and convenient for them as possible, make sure they had what they needed at both houses (no suitcases back and forth), and make sure they spent as much time as possible with both of us. To these ends, for the first four years of our separation and divorce, we lived only a block away from each other. Then, for about two years, the distance was a few miles. Currently, we live on the same street, with a short walk between houses. Such an arrangement may not be feasible for your family; aim to coordinate these co-parenting basics as best you can for your children, given your circumstances.

If you have not yet told the kids, agree on the dos and don'ts of telling them about the divorce or separation. Plan to tell them together, preferably after you've determined what your parenting time schedule will be upon separation, even if the schedule is just temporary. Agree in advance about what you will say—and what you won't say. Kids want to know how the separation and divorce will affect them—where they will live, whom they'll be with and when—not who's at fault or other grown-up matters. An excellent picture book to share with your kids is Mr. Rogers' *Let's Talk about It: Divorce* (Puffin, 1999). Also, see chapter 5 for more suggestions related to telling the kids about the divorce.

We strongly recommend not having this conversation with your children until after you've both consulted attorneys (or the same attorney; see chapter 3). For some parents, the legal and financial realities of divorce are a splash of cold water to the face, one that leads them to decide to postpone the divorce or take it off the table altogether. Others come away from a consultation with information that helps them make important decisions regarding their divorce, about when to file, parenting time, housing, money, and when to tell their children. If you're still weighing the question of whether or not to divorce, a helpful resource to consult is *Contemplating Divorce: A Step-by-Step Guide to Deciding Whether to Stay or Go* by Susan Pease Gadoua (New Harbinger Publications, 2008).

Commit to keeping your kids out of the revolving door of your dating lives. Some parents jump right into the dating scene during the divorce process. While that's their prerogative, grieving children shouldn't have new significant others thrust upon them, nor should they become attached to adults who may be in their lives only briefly. "Losing" someone this way can be heartbreaking for a child, further compounding feelings of loss related to the divorce. As a result, she may be reluctant to form or have difficulty forming close attachments in the future. Personally, we agreed that neither of us would introduce our children to anyone we dated unless and until we were as certain as we could be that this person was The One. (Ultimately, of our dating partners, our children only ever met the people who later became their stepparents.)

Some parents choose to specify a minimum amount of time dating a new partner as well as a minimum amount of time since the separation before introducing this person to the children—for example, after at least six months of dating, at least one year after the separation. Ron Deal, licensed marriage and family therapist and author of *The Smart Stepfamily*, estimates that even when adults feel ready to introduce children into their new partnerships, the children are actually not ready for such introductions until a year later (Philyaw, Thomas, and Mbonisi 2011).

If you are comfortable doing so, you might also agree that the other parent will be given the opportunity to meet your new significant other before you introduce him to the children.

Commit to avoid using legal means to right emotional wrongs. Recognize that by its very nature the court system is an adversarial process. In legal terms, divorce means one of you is actually suing the other. In such a system, one party "wins" and one party "loses"; applied to a family, however, no one really wins. In *The Smart Divorce*, divorced mom and divorce consultant Deborah Moskovitch (2007) writes about the importance of separating your "legal divorce" from your "emotional divorce." If either parent negotiates the divorce settlement agreement or re-litigates with "payback" or punishment in mind, or if either refuses to adhere to the agreement, the process drags on for longer and gets uglier than it needs to, delaying healing for all involved. Ultimately, then, the children are the ones who lose the most.

Planning for Future Peace

Making commitments such as these at the beginning of our separation helped us weather the divorce-related storms to come. It also contributed greatly to the peaceful parenting partnership we have today. The early commitments you make to your children can form the basis of your shared parenting agreement (aka parenting plan). These formal, written agreements are filed with the court in divorce cases as well as by never-married co-parents. Even in the most congenial co-parenting situation, having a written, legally enforceable agreement can minimize or alleviate future conflict over issues related to co-parenting (see chapter 8, "Write Your Own Parenting Plan").

Our experience and those of other cooperative co-parents prove that divorce with kids in the mix does not have to be an entirely acrimonious process. Instead of following the all-too-common scenario in which you and your soon-to-be ex rack up enormous lawyers' bills, chafe at every little offense (real or imagined), and fight just as much as (or more than) you did during the course of your relationship, why not plan to do everything you can to get through this difficult time as quickly and with as little drama as possible? If you can make your kids the top priority in your postdivorce relationship with your ex, you will be more likely to move on more quickly from the pain of divorce and less likely to damage your kids in the process. You'll be glad you did, and so will your children.

Even if you've already divorced, remember that co-parenting is a long-term undertaking, especially if your kids are young. Ongoing conflict is stressful and draining. Do you really want to commit at the outset to maintaining a combative posture for *years?* Whom does this serve? Certainly not your children, and ultimately not you either. So avoid decisions and behaviors that will serve to keep you and the other parent at odds. (If you, like many visitors to our website, are struggling to co-parent with a difficult ex, see chapter 12, "Fifteen Things You Can Do for Your Child in Spite of Your Uncooperative Ex.")

When parents commit to keeping their old intimate relationship and their new parenting partnership separate, and to keeping the vitriol and hurt from the former from tainting the latter, they lay the groundwork for co-parenting success. This, of course, is a tall order. We recommend counseling, divorce recovery groups, books like *Getting Divorced without Ruining Your Life: A Reasoned, Practical Guide to the Legal, Emotional, and Financial Ins and Outs of Negotiating a Divorce Settlement,* and online resources such as our blog *Co-Parenting 101,* Molly Monet's blog *Postcards from a Peaceful Divorce,* and the blog maintained by Mandy Walker, *Since My Divorce* (a complete list of resources can be found at the back of this book). We'll also talk about the process of moving on in chapter 2, "Good Grief: Strategies to Start the Healing Process."

Out of the Mouths of Babes: A Kid's-Eye View of Co-parenting

Co-parenting has been a journey of learning for us. We've read, talked, listened to others, and, most important, listened to our children. Our older daughter, Taylor, now fourteen, was six when we separated. She was ten when she agreed to grant us the following interview about co-parenting:

What is co-parenting?

Co-parenting is like trying to work with another parent, but not always being with them at the same time.

And when people co-parent, what are they working on?

They work on not always arguing, trying to get along, planning things to do with the kids, and not just thinking about how to get along, but also thinking about the kids and making sure they're okay and not worrying about their parents fighting all the time. But it's not *all* about the kids, because the parents need to be happy too.

Do you think co-parenting is easy or hard?

For some people it might be a little bit harder, especially if you broke up for a lot of different reasons and you broke up because of all the things going on. It was easier for my parents because they could control themselves. But some people make co-parenting harder because they want to prove they're better than the other parent or to make the other parent feel wrong. Some parents even want their kids to choose the better parent, and that makes it really hard on the child.

Why do you think it's important for parents to get along after divorce or another kind of breakup?

I think it's important to get along since after the breakup there's a lot of hurt feelings and sadness and confusion, and it makes it easier for the family to run smoothly if the parents get along. If the parents aren't getting along, it makes everything worse. Most kids dream about their parents getting back together, and having the parents get along is almost as good. Fighting and not getting along only make it worse for the kids.

Is there anything else you want to say?

I'm personally happy that my parents get along. I'm still upset that they got divorced, like a lot of kids. But I feel lucky that our family isn't as complicated as other families when there's divorce. Sometimes there's a lot of pain and confusion and a huge mess, like in the *Amber Brown* books [by Paula Danziger] I'm reading. Her [Amber Brown's] parents don't get along very well. Also, I want to say that I really wish that all families could get along with each other, but sometimes the world isn't like that, and sometimes the world is unfair.

But here's a tip for some parents to tell their kids, and for some kids to remember: You shouldn't keep your feelings about divorce all bottled up inside because that just makes you feel worse and worse, and someday it will just come exploding out in ways you never imagined. You shouldn't be afraid to talk to your parents about your feelings, no matter how embarrassed you might feel. It's better to be embarrassed than keep those feelings bottled up so much that you can't even enjoy the good things in life.

Chapter 2

Good Grief: Strategies to Start the Healing Process

[I learned that] I can't heal until I hurt. I had gone through the breakdown of my marriage with little emotion. Because the divorce was something I wanted in order to improve my life, I didn't feel much sadness. It took months until I felt the pain. And then I just resolved to feel it good. Real good. Gut-wrenching pain. Because I had to go there before I could get where I am today. It was part of the healing process—part of the self-repair.

—Lauren, mom of one

On airplanes, flight attendants routinely instruct parents to put on their own oxygen mask first, and then their children's, in the event of a loss of cabin pressure. A popular parenting metaphor uses this scenario to remind parents that in order to take good care of their children, they must first take care of themselves. For many families, divorce is an "emergency" of sorts, a time of crisis and grief during which both the parents' well-being and their children's is at stake. When mourning the end of an intimate relationship, and dealing with all the emotional and practical upheaval that comes with it, what form does the "oxygen mask" take for co-parents? They are called upon to offer their children a measure of emotional comfort, stability, and reassurance at precisely the time when their own emotional resources and reserves may be at an all-time low.

It's normal to grieve over a divorce. Elisabeth Kübler-Ross (1969) identified five stages of grief, in what is known as the Kübler-Ross grief cycle: denial, anger, bargaining, depression, and acceptance. Other grief process models expand on this to include hope (along with acceptance as a single stage), shock, guilt, and testing. Testing involves seeking realistic solutions to the problems related to your loss.

Kübler-Ross asserts (and we've observed anecdotally) that not everyone who grieves experiences all the above stages, nor do the stages necessarily occur in the order in which they're listed. Sometimes, people find themselves stuck in one or more stages. Note also that arriving at the acceptance and hope stage does not mean instant happiness. Whatever stages your process comprises, and however long it takes, don't fight it. Ride the waves of your grief toward the goal of coming out on the other side of it whole, prepared to move on and prepared to help your child move on as well. In chapter 5, we'll discuss ways to help your child through the grieving process.

Journaling through the Grief Process

Consider keeping a grief journal. In it, you can explore the thoughts and feelings—sometimes conflicting, sometimes overwhelming—you're experiencing as you transition from being partnered to being single again and as you begin parenting across two households.

Journaling can help minimize conflict because your feelings won't constantly be directed at your ex (or soon-to-be-ex)—or at your child.

A journal also provides a space for you to explore how the grief impacts you and your relationship with your child. Below are some ideas for journaling during each stage of the process.

Denial. Answer these questions in your journal to explore whether you have fully accepted the reality of your breakup and the changes that come with it:

+ Are you having difficulty accepting and admitting to yourself that your marriage is over?

+ Do you find yourself not wanting to deal with the logistics of the divorce and co-parenting arrangements?

+ Do you ignore or are you afraid to think about all the changes that are on the horizon for you and your child?

+ Are you holding out hope for reconciliation despite all indications of its unlikelihood?

Denial is often reported as the first stage of grief, though some people who continue to interact with their ex (such as co-parents) may experience this stage more than once. Co-parents who remain in denial are less effective at helping their children adjust to their new reality: living in two households with parents who are no longer in a relationship with each other. Down the road, these co-parents may also have difficulty accepting their ex's new significant other or spouse, which can make it difficult for their children to do so. Conversely, co-parents who are able to get past denial to acceptance can help their children do the same; then both parent and child are poised to begin adapting and healing.

Anger. This is an often overlooked or dreaded stage of grief. Anger can be scary because of the potential for loss of control. You may be angry at your partner, your partner's lover (in the case of an extramarital affair), your partner's parents, God (or the universe, or a higher power), life, or yourself for everything that has gone wrong. In your journal, write a letter in the voice of your anger. To whom is it addressed? What triggers your anger? What are some signs that let you know you're becoming angry?

Other strategies for defusing your anger are exercise, yoga, humor (read a funny book or watch a comedy), and relaxation techniques such as deep breathing and meditation.

For some co-parents, forgiving the other parent or forgiving themselves is central to working through their anger. You can read more about forgiveness later in this chapter and in chapter 6.

Though it is difficult, acknowledging their anger is for many co-parents essential to working through their grief. Repressed anger will continue to play itself out through the breakup and into the co-parenting arrangement, to the detriment of the children and the adults involved. Perpetually angry parents become difficult co-parents—interfering with the other parent's parenting time, bad-mouthing their ex to their kids, or acting passive-aggressively. By contrast, learning how to respond to anger and frustration in healthy ways facilitates healthy, cooperative co-parenting. Some co-parents turn to therapy and anger management classes to learn how to control their responses to anger and to address related sadness and depression.

Co-parents who admit their anger and work through it can also equip their children to safely address their anger about the divorce and its consequences. Children learn how to cope with negative emotions by observing their parents. What do you want to teach your child through your actions about how to handle anger and other strong feelings?

Bargaining. Do you find yourself bargaining with your partner, yourself, or a higher power to strike a deal, make concessions, or make promises—something, anything, to salvage or restore your relationship? Children who mistakenly believe that the divorce is their fault may also be inclined to bargain and try to negotiate their parents' divorce away. This is an opportunity to gently impress upon your child the permanent nature of divorce and to reiterate the fact that the divorce is in no way her fault.

Depression. Overwhelming sadness, anger, guilt, and feelings of powerlessness can lead to depression. One co-parenting mom told us of journaling: "I wrote my way through depression, during and after my divorce." On the advice of her therapist, this mom put her heavy thoughts and feelings into a journal instead of directing them at her ex-husband, breaking the cycle of bitter arguments that had plagued their parenting partnership.

Depression robs you of the physical, mental, and emotional energy you need to function. As a result, depression can hinder your ability to take care of obligations, including parenting. Like anger, depression must first be acknowledged before it can be addressed in healthy ways. The signs of depression are presented later in this chapter. Also, watch for any signs of depression in your child; take note of these, and consult your pediatrician or a family counselor.

Acceptance. Acceptance is the light at the end of what may feel like a never-ending tunnel when you are divorcing. You may go through the above stages multiple times, but with self-care, patience, honest introspection, and professional help as needed, you can make it. After a few months, revisit the pages of your journal to discover and appreciate just how far you've come, even if you're still working your way through the grief.

Steps toward Healing

Time alone doesn't heal all wounds, so even if your divorce or breakup happened a while ago, you may not have gone through the grieving process. How, then, can co-parents help themselves heal so that they can in turn help their children? Here are some suggestions:

Bury your intimate relationship and keep it separate from your new parenting partnership. Perhaps you're grieving the fact that your marriage or long-term relationship is over. Or perhaps you're grieving because of the emotional and logistical fallout from the relationship's ending, including the impact on your children. Cooperative co-parenting is possible when you allow yourself to grieve and put this relationship to rest.

At the same time that you're burying this relationship, your post-breakup parenting partnership is being born. Imagine that your "dead" relationship is a zombie, threatening the newborn infant that is your post-breakup parenting partnership. Protect the partnership just as you would that infant. Keep them separate and apart, so that the parenting partnership has a chance to thrive, untainted by any residual bitterness and unresolved hurts from the old relationship. Vent about your ex only when your children aren't around, and don't burden your children with details about money and other problems related to the breakup. As stepmom Izzy Rose (2009) observes in her book *The Package Deal: My (Not-So) Glamorous Transition from Single Gal to Instant Mom*, our children should never be our "emotional bellhops" (231).

In the wake of a breakup, you may rightfully feel that your ex abandoned you and your relationship. This does not mean, however, that she has abandoned your child or forfeited her parental rights. When parents fail to compartmentalize in this way, co-parenting becomes a new battleground on which to fight an old war, and children are the casualties.

For over five years, Corey, a co-parenting dad, has dealt with an ex-wife who still hasn't let go of hurts from their marriage. "She hates me, so she thinks the kids should hate me too. She tries to keep them from spending time with me, and she doesn't want me at our daughter's swim meets. But my daughter wants me there, and that's all that matters to me. My ex says that I made her life hell by leaving and filing for divorce, so she's going to make *my* life hell now every chance she gets. But when she bad-mouths me, says the kids don't need me, and doesn't stick to the parenting time schedule, our kids suffer most."

Instead of continuing to grind an ax of complaints from the relationship, or anger about the breakup, focus on meeting your child's needs, without confusing these with your adult wants. Like Corey's ex, you may wish your child's other parent would fall off the face of the earth. But this isn't what your child wants or needs.

Try seeing through your child's eyes. Even co-parents who are committed to keeping the peace may still feel strong emotions related to the breakup. When you feel overwhelmed by anger, frustration, or hurt, remember that while you may view your ex as the enemy, your child does not share your sentiment and has a right to enjoy a loving relationship with both parents. *The D-Word: Divorce Through a Child's Eyes* by Tara Eisenhard is narrated by 12-year-old Gina. Gina's stroy reveals how well-meaning parents and unbridled emotions can compound the fear, confusion, and hurt children experience in the wake of divorce.

Think of the other parent less as "my ex" and more as "my co-parent" (in this book, we switch freely between "your ex" and "your co-parent"). Civil and cooperative co-parenting limits your child's exposure to parental conflict and frees him to love both parents without feeling pressure to declare loyalty to one or the other. Look through your child's eyes, and you may see the other parent in a more forgiving light.

Seek therapeutic or spiritual counseling. Divorce and separation can take a social, emotional, financial, and sometimes even physical toll on a parent—even the parent who initiated the proceedings. Don't hesitate to seek professional help, especially if you find yourself unable to move through the stages of grief. If you pray or have another spiritual practice, do it.

Also seek help if you find that over time you can't shake your angry or sad feelings about your breakup or toward your ex, or if these unresolved feelings are interfering with your ability to co-parent civilly or effectively.

Surround yourself with positive people who care about you and your children. Reach out to affirming friends and relatives. Uncle Lou, who spoils your kids rotten and loves you unconditionally, is a better choice than Aunt Betty, who thinks your ex is evil incarnate and says so every chance she gets. Seek out an informal or formal divorce support group, such as Divorce Care. Too often, the shame and guilt associated with divorce keep those in need from finding comfort among their loved ones.

Take care of your basic needs. In the midst of the upheaval that comes with separation and divorce, it's very easy to forget the obvious, especially as a parent. Eat well. Get enough sleep. Exercise. Drink plenty of water.

Beware of divorce guilt. In the early stages of divorce and postdivorce, many co-parents indulge their children with gifts or by being overly permissive in an effort to "make up for" the divorce or assuage their guilt about it. Just as you can't punish your ex forever, you can't pay penance to your children forever. Plus, indulgence keeps your children from learning coping skills and from adapting to the changes in their lives. If you're tempted to give your kids extra anything, make it extra time and extra hugs. See chapter 6 for more on divorce guilt.

Call in the reinforcements: grandparents, friends, neighbors, playdates. Declare a kid-free day or weekend for yourself: Sleep in. Veg. Ignore the laundry. Rest your body and your mind.

Familiarize yourself with the signs and symptoms of depression. These include considerable change in appetite (increased or decreased); significant weight loss or weight gain; sleep difficulties (insomnia or oversleeping); difficulty focusing; and feelings of hopelessness or worthlessness. If these symptoms significantly interfere with your life, or if you are having thoughts of harming yourself or others, seek treatment.

Clean house. Literally. Do your best to de-clutter and let go of any painful reminders of the relationship that has ended. However, don't be too quick to toss your wedding photos or group family photos; your children may continue to cherish these. Our daughters chose to keep our wedding album, and they display pre-divorce family photos, as well as photos from our wedding and honeymoon, in their bedrooms.

Treat yourself. Money may be too tight for a spa day—divorce is certainly not the best time for extensive "retail therapy" and living beyond your means—but you can check out some new books, rent a movie, get a haircut, or organize a potluck dinner or zoo outing with friends or other single and newly single parents whom you know.

Resist the urge to fall immediately into another intimate relationship. Regardless of how lonely and neglected you may feel in the wake of the breakup, chances are you're not ready for a new relationship. Getting involved with someone else is an easy but unwise means of filling an emotional void and masking your grief and pain. Some co-parents, understandably eager to embrace their life's second act, may rush to find a new partner, or they may neglect their responsibilities in order to hit the dating scene with a vengeance. This is a tempting escape, especially when you feel overwhelmed, but ultimately, it hinders the healing process.

Hooking up with someone new in order to make your ex jealous or to get back at him is also a bad idea, not to mention terribly unfair to the new person. More important, your child, who is also grieving, is certainly not ready to meet your new love interest.

Finally, even if you were already involved with someone else before your relationship ended, it's advisable to take a step back and take a break between relationships. We've heard from co-parents in this situation that, even if they initiated the divorce, they still found themselves needing to grieve.

Give it time. Just as you owe it to yourself and your children not to jump into a new relationship, you owe it to yourself and your children to give the healing process time. How you are feeling and interacting with your ex may change six months or a year from now. Allow for that change, and show your ex and your children the same patience and grace as they heal. We hear from some co-parents that it took years before they (or their ex) turned a corner in their parenting partnerships from hostility or cold war to civility and, in some cases, friendship.

Debbie, a co-parenting mom, told us how her chest would tighten every time her ex walked into her house to pick up their son. His presence brought back sad feelings and memories of when they all lived in the house together. She even considered having their son meet his dad outside on the steps, so that she could avoid the awkwardness. But she didn't want to have to explain to her son that his father was no longer welcome in the house. Instead, she decided to grin and bear it until one day, after her son and his dad had left, she realized that her chest hadn't tightened. Debbie took comfort in this small milestone in her healing journey.

Forgive. For many co-parents, this is the final step in the grieving process, and it's a long time in coming. For others, it never comes. Some won't let go of the hurt and anger, for fear that forgiveness means letting the other parent "off the hook" for bad behavior in the marriage. But as Becca, a co-parenting mom of three, found out, "Forgiveness doesn't make the other person right. It sets you free." And in co-parenting situations, when you forgive, you are modeling the concept of forgiveness for your child.

You can't commit to honoring your child's relationship with the other parent *and* commit to punishing that parent forever at the same time. Guess which "commitment" has to go. Forgiveness doesn't have to involve an explicit conversation with the other parent. It's an act of healing for you as much as it is for the other person, if not more so. To withhold forgiveness is to carry a burden. Saint Augustine said it plainly: "Resentment is like taking poison and hoping the other person dies." Living well—being positive, focused, and free of the weight of a dead relationship—truly is the best revenge.

Think forgiveness is too hard, or what your ex did is unforgivable? Consider the story of Alece Ronzino, a former missionary whose husband asked for a divorce after having an affair with her friend. Ronzino blogs about her emotional journey at gritandglory. com. In processing her grief, she found that "The only thing harder on your heart than forgiveness is unforgiveness" (2010).

For more on forgiveness, including the importance of forgiving yourself, see chapter 6.

Read books and consult other resources. There is a plethora of resources available to help you in your healing process. *How to Heal a Broken Heart in 30 Days* by Mike Riley and Howard Bronson and *The Good Karma Divorce* by Michele Lowrance are two helpful books. Lowrance is a family court judge who champions a non-adversarial approach to divorce and co-parenting. Another worthy resource we've found is a series of recovery exercises called the Phoenix Ritual, available for free at newlifeafterdivorce.com, a website that also features articles, tips, and more. Just as the legendary phoenix rose from the ashes to live again, it is possible for you to emerge whole after divorce.

If All Else Fails, Remember: "It's Not about You"

"It's not about you" is *Co-Parenting 101*'s tough-love catchphrase, our fallback when co-parents tell us they just can't let go of drama with the ex. We can talk about righteous anger, pain, embarrassment, and disappointment in the wake of divorce or separation. But when children are involved, there comes a time when co-parents have to put on their big-girl panties or big-boy boxers and pull themselves together, for their kids' sake. Children's author Susan McKenna (n.d.) describes this struggle:

> Adults need to basically split into two people. One of those personalities has to work on getting through the adult stages of divorce [grief]…as well as rebuilding their self image ….
> That can be very grueling and emotional; however, if children are involved, it is even more difficult. *A second personality has to be concerned with the total needs of the child.*
> When children are part of the divorce, it can either be a motivator to get back on track or a roadblock…
>
> Parents must be open and accepting to the fact that they and their children are still a family, even if there is not a

biological mother and father under one roof after divorce. Sometimes parents hold onto the opposite belief and never stop mourning the loss of a two-parent home, then use that loss as the basis for what happens or doesn't happen moving forward. [emphasis ours]

Meeting your own needs in the wake of divorce or separation while also meeting those of your kids is a tremendous and heartbreaking challenge, particularly in the early days. Some parents never move past the grief and anger. Maybe this is why they conflate their children's feelings with their own: *If I'm mad at Mommy, you should be too*, or *If I can't stand interacting with Daddy, then I'm going to minimize his parenting time or keep him from seeing you altogether.*

Few co-parents articulate these thoughts outright (though some do), but behavior speaks volumes. Co-parents who are mired in their own "stuff" appear oblivious to their kids' emotional needs and feelings related to the divorce and to the fact that these needs and feelings are separate and likely very different from their own.

Parenting, functioning, staying sane, and meeting your child's needs in the wake of a divorce or separation—it's all an enormous challenge. But not an insurmountable one. We titled this chapter "Good Grief" because while divorce is a traumatic experience for both children and adults, the grieving process, if undertaken, is a good step toward healing and stability. Counseling, self-care, the passage of time, and a strong commitment to your children's well-being all help shift the focus from the past to the co-parenting you must do in the present and the future.

There are many things you can't give your children in the wake of a divorce, such as both parents living under the same roof and many other aspects of life as they once knew it. But what *is* absolutely in your power is giving your children as much peace, peace of mind, and reassurance as possible. So strap on your postdivorce oxygen mask, and then strap on your child's. In doing so, you give your child the fresh air of unconditional love, comfort, hope, and truth, not the toxic fumes of self-pity, blame, unresolved anger, and pessimism.

There's a saying that goes, "Hurt people hurt people." In the darkest of times, parents can inadvertently hurt their children with their own unresolved grief, when truly what the children need most is hope. As a parent, it's your job to lead yourself out of darkness so that you can give your children that hope. However, if your children manage to see light at the end of the tunnel and a glimmer of happiness with their other parent in the midst of the tough times, you must allow them to move forward in this way.

In the meantime, your own plate is full, with not only the emotional work of the grief process but also the legal and practical matters related to co-parenting and divorce. In the next chapter, we'll explore the steps involved in formalizing your new parenting partnership.

Chapter 3

Attorneys and Mediators and Collaborative Divorce—Oh, My!

A lawyer is never entirely comfortable with a
friendly divorce, any more than a good
mortician wants to finish his job and then have
the patient sit up on the table.

—Jean Kerr, author of *Please Don't Eat the Daisies*

Retaining legal representation in the form of a divorce or family law attorney is often the first official step parents take in the divorce process. However, for those co-parents who anticipate a "simple" divorce—that is, little or no disagreements about parenting time or support and an uncomplicated property and asset split—this chapter explores the cost-saving options of using a mediator in lieu of an attorney; sharing a single attorney; and collaborative divorce, a conflict-resolution approach to divorce in which both parties agree not to go to court, nor to threaten to do so.

The following sections will help you assess which options are viable in your particular circumstances. And in case you do decide to retain separate divorce attorneys, we'll share some qualities to look for when selecting a lawyer who will facilitate, not stand in the way of, your successful parenting partnership.

Mediation

Depending on state law, at least one session with a mediator may be a mandatory part of your divorce proceedings. But some parents choose to use a mediator to facilitate *all* their negotiations, instead of hiring attorneys or litigating pro se (without representation). In divorce mediation, a trained, qualified mediator (sometimes an attorney) acts as a neutral third party to assist the divorcing parents in reaching agreement on matters related to parenting time, child support, alimony, and division of assets. The mediator cannot advocate for or give legal advice to either parent. Unlike judges, mediators have no decision-making power. Some co-parents choose mediation precisely because it allows them to maintain control over important matters impacting their children, such as parenting time.

The absence of lawyers makes mediation a faster, less adversarial approach to divorce—and a cheaper one. According to the Boston Law Cooperative, the average cost of divorce mediation is $6,600, compared to $26,830 on average for lawyer-negotiated divorce and $77,746 on average for traditional family court divorce litigation (Neil 2007). But while divorce mediation may be a workable solution for some co-parents, there are some potential drawbacks to consider:

1. Mediation requires a lot of preparation and information- and document-gathering on the part of both parents.

2.   Without legal advice, one or both parents may fail to act in their own or their children's best interest, short-term or long-term. The amount of time and money saved by mediating today may pale in comparison to time and money spent going back to court later to correct or modify the previously negotiated settlement. While some aspects of the agreement, such as child support, may be modified through the courts at a later date, others, such as alimony, typically cannot. For this reason, some divorcing parties who choose mediation also consult with attorneys (at an hourly rate, instead of paying a large retainer) to find out their legal options, for settlement ideas, and for coaching through the negotiations.

3.   Successful mediation requires both parties to be reasonable and flexible—willing to negotiate—advocate for themselves, and maintain self-control. The mediator can attempt to get a derailed mediation back on track, but without the cooperation of the parties, the process may break down.

4.   The mediator can end a session that becomes unproductive or volatile, but she cannot force either parent to agree to anything or to reach a settlement.

Mediation works best for those who are (a) able to gather and organize the many documents needed to create and finalize a settlement agreement; (b) willing to remain civil and cooperative during the process; and (c) generally in agreement about custody and parenting time issues.

Collaborative Divorce

While the term may sound like an oxymoron, collaborative divorce is a viable option for couples who aren't equipped or prepared to advocate for themselves in mediation. At an average cost of just under $20,000 (about a quarter of the cost of traditional divorce litigation), a collaborative divorce is executed by a team of specially trained lawyers, financial analysts, and mental health and child specialists. Like a mediated divorce, collaborative divorce focuses on the singular goal of a divorce settlement agreed upon by both parties. Unlike in a mediated divorce, in a collaborative divorce the parties have separate attorneys to represent and advocate for them and provide legal advice.

Here's how the collaborative process typically works:

1. Both parties and their respective attorneys agree, in writing, to negotiate a settlement without litigation or the threat of litigation. If either side violates this agreement, the process is terminated and both attorneys are barred from representing their clients in any subsequent litigated case.

2. Both sides—clients and attorneys—promise to be reasonable, cooperative, honest, and respectful and to operate in good faith during negotiations.

3. While each party retains an attorney to represent solely his or her interest, both attorneys are charged with working in good faith to find mutually agreeable terms for the settlement, instead of holding out for the largest possible settlement for his or her client as is common in traditional divorce litigation.

4. Attorneys must act with integrity and refrain from using threat, deception, intimidation, or other adversarial tactics during the proceedings.

5. Financial analysts, mental health professionals, and child development experts are engaged as needed while the parties work out the financial and child-related terms of their settlement.

6. If one of the parties decides to abandon the process in favor of going through the court system, both attorneys are obligated to withdraw from the case. The desire to avoid the

expense of hiring new counsel gives the parties an incentive to stay the course and negotiate.

Critics of collaborative divorce argue that the process may pressure some parties to agree to a settlement that they don't really want. In order to avoid starting the negotiation process all over again—and paying to retain a new lawyer on top of the fees already paid to the collaborative team—a parent might agree to terms that are not in his or the children's best interest.

In our opinion, collaborative divorce is nonetheless a good option for those who seek a congenial, respectful resolution but who may have complicated legal, financial, and parenting time issues to work out.

Sharing an Attorney

"[My husband] Terry and I sat down and had a heart-to-heart. Several heart-to-hearts, actually," said Christina, a co-parenting mom of two middle-schoolers. "I said, 'Look, I'm not trying to screw you out of any money, the kids need both of us in their lives, and it's in everybody's best interest that we not spend a ton on lawyers' fees. Let's try and do this as cheaply as possible.' So, he agreed, and we hired one attorney to help us finalize everything." Christina and Terry encountered some tough negotiations when it came to splitting assets, but they were on the same page with regard to their parenting time schedule. They decided on a nesting arrangement (see chapter 7), and with the negotiations behind them, they moved on to the first step in their co-parenting journey: telling their children about the divorce.

Sharing an attorney worked for Christina and Terry, but consider these factors before deciding to go this route:

1. Your state's laws may forbid attorneys from representing both parties in a divorce. According to its publication *Model Rules of Professional Conduct*, the American Bar Association discourages shared representation except in cases where the

attorney "will be able to provide competent and diligent representation to each affected client" (ABA Center for Professional Responsibility 2010). Make sure your attorney has prior experience working in this capacity with other couples.

2.   As with mediation, the time and money you save by sharing an attorney may not be worth it if you end up with a child support or alimony arrangement that turns out to be inadequate to meet your needs or your children's needs. A compromise made while working with a shared attorney may not be in your or your children's best interest in the long run. By sharing an attorney, you forfeit the benefits of having someone advocating solely in your best interest. How will your shared attorney proceed if your interest conflicts with your soon-to-be-ex's interest?

3.   Disagreements about parenting time can be especially contentious. Sharing an attorney is not recommended if you and your co-parent don't see eye-to-eye on these issues.

Choosing Separate Attorneys

If you think the issues in your divorce may be too complicated for the two of you to use a mediator or share an attorney, or if you anticipate an ugly fight with your soon-to-be-ex about custody or money, get an attorney. Some co-parents tell us that they felt so emotionally overwhelmed, confused, or defeated at the outset of their divorce that they just wanted the process to be over. So they failed to retain an attorney (or chose one haphazardly) and later regretted it. Divorce is a legal process. In fact, we were surprised to learn that in court documents and legalese, the person initiating the proceedings is considered the plaintiff and is *suing* the other spouse—the defendant—for divorce, even if the case doesn't go to trial. So, as with any other complex legal matter, a good attorney can educate you and save you time, stress, and possibly money (counterintuitive, we know) in the long run. A good attorney can help you avoid lost time at work due to repeat court visits later to attempt to modify an unfair or inadequate settlement or alimony or child support allocation.

Don't allow the cost of representation to deter you from seeking it. Many attorneys accept credit cards or will set up payment plans. It won't help your kids for you to bankrupt yourself paying for a divorce, but you also don't want to shortchange yourself or them in the grand scheme of things.

So how do you go about choosing an attorney who's a good fit for your situation? Do your homework, because all attorneys are not created equal.

"At the first consultation, I told my attorney that even though my wife had had an affair, I had no intention of using that against her in the divorce. I knew that an ugly divorce would hurt my kids," said Marlon, a divorced dad of two daughters. "Well, the attorney was downright disappointed when I told her that I wasn't interested in fighting dirty, or fighting period. She agreed to retract her fangs for my case, but after that, she was lax and halfhearted in advocating for me. The bigger the fight, the longer the process takes, and the more money she stood to make. So since my case wasn't a 'big fight,' I wasn't a priority. I probably should have changed attorneys, but I didn't because I was just too drained to start all over again."

Dara, a co-parenting mom of twins, had the opposite experience: "My attorney complimented my soon-to-be-ex and me on making our children's best interest our top priority. Nobody was interested in a custody battle, and my attorney went as far as saying that she viewed going to court as a failure. She set the goal for us to negotiate everything with my ex and his attorney, so that we could make important decisions for our kids—not some judge. And in the end, my ex and I never set foot inside a courtroom. Everything was finalized by the attorneys on our behalf.... While we did have a bumpy start at co-parenting, having the legal stuff go relatively smoothly helped us be there for our kids in a way that we couldn't have been if we'd still been fighting over every little thing in court."

To find an attorney like Dara's (and avoid ones like Marlon's), here are some questions to ask yourself or prospective attorneys when you interview them:

1. **Does the attorney have any potential conflict of interest with regard to your case?** For example, does he know your spouse?

2. **Does the attorney know your spouse's attorney's reputation?** For example, if opposing counsel is known for using hardball tactics in divorce litigation, your attorney should be aware of this and prepared to represent your interest under these circumstances.

3. **Does the attorney support your desire to avoid a contentious divorce?**

4. **Does the attorney support your desire to share custody and co-parent cooperatively?** Beware of attorneys who have opinions or biases that can undermine your parenting partnership, such as "As a father, you shouldn't expect to get much more than weekends with your kids," "It's too confusing for kids to go back and forth between houses," "You'll get more in child support if you sue for sole custody," "I don't believe in alimony," or "You're their mother, so you should have primary custody." You want to be represented by someone who shares your values as they relate to co-parenting and divorce and who won't needlessly antagonize your spouse. So don't hesitate to ask for the attorney's personal opinions on these issues.

5. **Are you and your soon-to-be-ex generally in agreement about child support, custody, parenting time, assets, and money matters?** If so, an attorney who is a strong negotiator and who prefers to mediate and negotiate rather than go to court would be a good fit for you. If not, and especially if either of you is seeking sole physical or legal custody over the objections of the other, you'll need to find an attorney

who is prepared to litigate your case. (For the difference between physical and legal custody, see chapter 7.)

6. **Are assets like property, cash, stock options, and retirement plans a part of your divorce settlement? Will alimony or business valuation be a factor in your case?** Does the attorney work with accountants and other specialists when necessary? Give the attorney as much information as possible about the issues you think will come up in your case, and make sure the attorney you choose has experience negotiating such matters.

7. **Does your case involve domestic violence, child abuse (or allegations of such), substance abuse, mental illness, or a parent or child with special needs or disabilities?** Make the attorney aware of any special circumstances in your case, and ask whether she has experience representing clients with similar profiles.

8. **Is the attorney familiar with local family court judges and their dispositions?** Once your case has been assigned to a judge, an attorney who knows that judge's reputation and disposition can prepare accordingly. For example, if a judge has a known disliking for piles of documentation and lengthy motions, a good attorney will understand the need to present your case as succinctly as possible.

9. **Does the attorney have a heavy caseload—if so, will anyone else in the firm be involved in your case? What is this person's experience level? Will you communicate primarily via phone or e-mail?** An overextended, incompetent, or unresponsive attorney can cost you time (which translates to money), jeopardize the outcome of your negotiations, and add stress to an already stressful situation.

10. **Will the attorney ask for your input before planning or executing a strategy?** It's important that your attorney have your buy-in before acting on your behalf. While you'll

certainly respect her expertise, remember that it's you and your children, not the attorney, who must live with the outcome of your case.

11. **Will the attorney keep you apprised of developments in your case and make sure you have copies of all documents related to your case, including documents filed with the court and all communication with your spouse's attorney?** You'll need these documents for your personal files, and you'll need them if you decide to change attorneys later.

12. **What fees and costs are involved?** A reputable attorney will provide a contract outlining the fee arrangement and will discuss the following with you: the amount of his retainer; his hourly rate; fees for the services of associates who work on the cases; fees for specialists, such as accountants; court fees in the case of litigation; itemized billing; status updates on the retainer; option of petitioning the court for your spouse to pay for your attorney fees; billing for phone calls and letters; fees for copies of documents; and other costs, such as court filing fees and process server fees. Some of these fees may not apply to your case; be sure to ask about fees and billing up front so you know what to expect. Divorce is an expensive undertaking, financially as well as emotionally. Educating yourself about the process and costs involved can help you avoid feeling overwhelmed or blindsided later.

If You've Already Finalized Your Divorce

If you've already finalized your divorce, you can't rely on the courts to right all wrongs; however, if you feel as though you were treated unfairly in your divorce proceedings or if you wish to modify your agreement, a mediator or an attorney can help you explore your options.

Whichever approach you and your co-parent take to complete your divorce, remember that conducting yourselves as adversaries during the process will make building a good parenting partnership difficult. Difficult, but not impossible. In the next chapter, we provide a quiz for you to assess your co-parenting style and see where there is room to build a stronger parenting team with your ex.

Part II

Co-parenting Basics

Once you have paved the way for cooperative co-parenting during and immediately following your divorce or separation, what are the next steps, the fundamentals of co-parenting? In this part of the book, we'll lay out the basic rules of engagement, the to-do lists, and the "do" and "don't" lists that enable co-parents to minimize conflict with each other and make life as peaceful as possible for their children during this time of transition and emotional upheaval—and beyond. We'll start by assessing your co-parenting style. What is your present approach to co-parenting? What are the rewards and potential pitfalls of this approach?

Chapter 4

What's Your
Co-parenting Style?

I'd say we're probably somewhere between Bruce and Demi,
and Alec Baldwin and Kim Basinger. We're not all vacationing
together, but nobody is calling and cussing on the phone
either. It's a happy medium for everybody.

—Talia, describing her co-parenting
relationship with her ex-boyfriend

Co-parenting is not a one-size-fits-all proposition. Individual personalities, temperaments, and quirks; the reasons for the breakup; the
nature of the breakup; the ages of the children; the children's reactions to the divorce; socioeconomic realities; the way the divorce proceedings played out; the presence of a new significant other; the
influence of the "supporting cast" of friends and relatives—all these
factors inform how you and your ex interact as co-parents.

"The Co-parenting Quiz," below, will help you identify your co-parenting style. This quiz will assess whether you and your parenting partner are "Super Friends," whose co-parenting relationship is characterized by low conflict, flexibility, easy communication, and congeniality; "Business Partners," characterized by more formal interaction, strict adherence to schedules and written plans, and a basic civility; or "Oil and Water," characterized by a near or total breakdown of communication, high conflict, mistrust, and competitiveness. After scoring your quiz and determining your style, read on to find out the pros and cons of each of these approaches.

The Co-parenting Quiz: What's Your Co-parenting Style?

For each item below, choose the answer that best reflects your true feelings and experiences. Don't worry about the "best" or "right" answer. Your honest answer is the right one, because taking an honest look at your current co-parenting style will allow you to make positive changes going forward. Note: Your co-parenting style is a reflection of your own intentions, outlook, and actions as a co-parent. In some cases, your co-parenting style may be different from that of the other parent.

Communicating with the Kids

How you talk about the other parent and the divorce with your child can influence the grieving process for your family.

1. Which statement best describes how you feel (or felt) about discussing the divorce with your children?

    a. My children deserve to know the whole truth about why my ex and I broke up, even if it embarrasses my ex or shatters the image they have of her.

    b. My children deserve to know only age-appropriate information, even if it's not the entire truth.

    c. My children deserve to hear both sides of the story of why we broke up, straight from the horse's mouth.

2. Regarding bad-mouthing the other parent in front of the kids or allowing others to do so:

    a. I don't think there's anything wrong with it.

    b. I've never done it or allowed it.

    c. I used to, but I make sure it doesn't happen anymore.

Communicating and Interacting with Your Co-parent

Effective, respectful communication is central to a successful parenting partnership. Also, how you communicate and interact with your ex influences how your children view conflict resolution and problem solving.

3. I *would prefer to* communicate with my co-parent regarding our children's education, extracurricular activities, and overall well-being:

    a. informally, as often as is necessary.

    b. on a regular schedule (e.g., weekly, monthly, three times a year).

    c. rarely, if at all.

4. If my co-parent and I are having difficulty communicating, I usually:

    a. convey important messages to her through our children.

    b. use text, e-mail, or a third party in order to minimize conflict.

    c. work through the difficulty face-to-face or on the phone.

5. When our children are with me:

    a. they communicate with the other parent via phone, e-mail, text messages, or other means, either informally or at scheduled times.

    b. I do not allow them to communicate with the other parent.

    c. they communicate with the other parent, but I wish they wouldn't.

6. Which statement best describes how you support your children's relationship with the other parent?

   a. I refrain from bad-mouthing him. I do not make negative comments, roll my eyes, or otherwise discourage the children from talking about him, loving him, and wanting to spend time with him.

   b. It's not in my children's best interest to have a close relationship with my co-parent, so I don't support it.

   c. I neither encourage nor discourage the relationship my children have with my co-parent. That relationship is her responsibility.

7. Which statement best describes how you feel about vacationing with your co-parent?

   a. I would never consider vacationing together with my ex and our children.

   b. My co-parent and I have vacationed together with our children.

   c. In the future, I might consider vacationing together with my ex and our children.

8. Which statement best describes your experience of conflict with your co-parent?

   a. There will always be conflict between us.

   b. Our conflict is more of a cold war—not heated, but there's definitely tension beneath the surface.

   c. It's not always easy, but we try to deal constructively with conflict as it arises.

9. Which statement best describes how you and your co-parent handle conflicts in front of your children?

   a. We rarely interact, so we have few if any conflicts or disagreements.

   b. Our children are aware that sometimes we have conflicts or disagreements, and they see us managing them appropriately.

c. It's no secret that we don't get along, so our children are fully aware of our conflicts and disagreements.

10. With regard to respect:

   a. my children should respect my co-parent, and I model this respect myself.

   b. whether or not the children respect my ex is none of my concern.

   c. because of his failings and shortcomings, my ex is not due any respect from the children.

11. Which statement best describes how you view communicating with your ex about your child?

   a. We're a parenting team. We share important information and observations about our child with each other.

   b. Parents should trust the other parent and thus should concern themselves with what's going on with their children only during their designated parenting time.

   c. There's no reason for my ex to inquire about my children when they are with me, but it's important for me to know what goes on when they are with him.

12. If my children tell me that something upsetting or unpleasant happened during their time with the other parent, first I address my children's needs and feelings, then I usually:

   a. decide whether the issue warrants a call to my co-parent. If it does, I try to discuss the matter without putting him on the defensive.

   b. confront my co-parent about the matter.

   c. say nothing to my co-parent, but keep a mental or written note about these kinds of incidents.

Schedules and Parenting Time

It's in a child's best interest to spend meaningful time with both parents if they are fit and willing. A parenting time schedule helps ensure that children have this time and are able to stay connected to both parents.

13. Regarding parenting time:

    a. our children should have as much parenting time as is feasible with each of us, allowing for a flexible schedule as needed.

    b. it's in our children's best interest to spend all or the majority of their time with me.

    c. we should have equal amounts of parenting time, according to a set schedule.

14. Which statement best describes your thoughts regarding co-parenting and your children's education?

    a. My ex should have no input on homework and school projects when the kids are with me.

    b. When it comes to homework and school projects, both parents should participate based on the children's needs, not just the parenting time schedule.

    c. There's no need for my ex to be involved at all with the children's schoolwork or parent-teacher conferences.

15. With regard to discipline:

    a. even when our approach to discipline differs, I respect my co-parent's right to discipline our children during her parenting time, and we can discuss these issues if the need arises.

    b. my children know I disagree with my co-parent's approach to discipline, and it helps them to know that I'm on their side.

    c. how we each discipline during our parenting time is none of the other parent's business, as long as the children are treated well.

16. Regarding our parenting plan (formal or informal):

    a. I adhere to it without exception.

    b. I am willing to be flexible as plans change unexpectedly and as our children's needs change.

    c. I am violating the plan, and it is a source of conflict.

17. On our child's birthday, I'd like to celebrate by having my co-parent and myself:

    a. alternate years (take turns) organizing parties that we both attend.

    b. organize separate parties (or one of us organizes a party), and we do not attend the party the other parent hosts.

    c. organize the party together.

New Partners

The introduction of a new significant other can place a strain on a previously stable parenting partnership or exacerbate existing tensions. The way parents conduct themselves during this new chapter in their co-parenting experience can impact their children's ability to adjust to the change.

18. If I plan to introduce a new partner to my children:

    a. it's none of my ex's concern; I may or may not mention it to him after the fact.

    b. I will make my ex aware of it before I make the introduction.

    c. I will make my ex aware of it before I make the introduction and give her the opportunity to meet my new partner.

19. If I were to learn that my ex was dating or had remarried:

    a. I'd be concerned, either because he might try to replace me as a parent or because I don't trust his judgment.

    b. my only interest and concern would be our children's well-being.

    c. I'd be interested because my children's well-being is a factor, but I'd also be happy for her.

Processing Emotions around the Divorce

Your postdivorce parenting partnership will be shaped in part by how you work through your feelings about the breakup. At the same time, your children will need you to help them work through their feelings. We've learned from adults whose parents divorced that a co-parent's emotional journey can make a lasting impression on a child—one that continues into adulthood—and can directly impact the child's ability to thrive after the divorce.

20. Which statement best describes how you feel about your ex?

    a. I no longer trust or respect my co-parent as a mate, and he is no longer worthy of my trust and respect as a parent.

    b. While I may regard my ex through the lens of our breakup, I respect that our children still see her as a loving parent.

    c. I no longer trust my ex, and I've warned my children about him.

21. Which statement best describes how the specific circumstances of your divorce influence your attitude and willingness to co-parent?

    a. Issues related to alimony, child support, property settlement, the reasons for the divorce, or other breakup-related matters have made co-parenting more challenging for me than it might otherwise be.

    b. The specific circumstances surrounding our divorce have made it impossible for me to co-parent.

    c. My commitment to cooperative co-parenting is unconditional.

22. Which statement best describes how you feel about co-parenting with your ex?

    a. Having to co-parent with my ex is a constant struggle because of my feelings toward him.

    b. Regardless of how I feel about my ex and regardless of how she acts, I keep things civil for our children's sake.

    c. I like my ex and we get along well as parenting partners.

23. On holidays involving gift exchange and on the other parent's birthday:

    a. I help my children purchase or make gifts for the other parent.

    b. my children don't want to give the other parent gifts, and I don't insist on it.

    c. if my children make or purchase gifts for the other parent, I do not assist or encourage them in any way.

24. If asked to describe our co-parenting relationship today, our child would say:

    a. "My parents get along okay" or "My parents are still friendly."

    b. "My parents hate each other."

    c. "One of my parents hates the other."

25. Ten or twenty years from now, I believe our children will say:

    a. "Our parents broke up, and they never got along after that."

    b. "Our parents broke up and didn't interact much after that, but they never made us feel as though we had to choose sides."

    c. "Our parents broke up, but they worked as a team to take care of us."

Score Your Quiz

In the chart below, for each question, circle the number that corresponds to your answer of a, b, or c; total the circled numbers in each column; then add these three numbers together for your score.

Question #	a	b	c
1	5	1	5
2	5	1	3
3	1	3	5
4	5	3	1
5	1	5	3
6	1	5	3
7	5	1	3
8	5	3	1
9	3	1	5
10	1	3	5
11	1	3	5
12	1	5	3
13	1	5	3
14	3	1	5
15	1	5	3
16	3	1	5
17	1	5	1
18	5	1	1
19	5	3	1
20	5	1	5
21	3	5	1
22	5	3	1
23	1	5	5
24	1	5	5
25	5	3	1
Totals:	_____ +	_____ +	_____ = Score _____

If your score is 25–34, your co-parenting style is *Super Friends*.

If your score is 35–95, your co-parenting style is *Business Partners*.

If your score is 96–125, your co-parenting style is *Oil and Water*.

Super Friends

You understand that parents are parents 24/7, not just during their scheduled parenting time, and you consider yourself an active member of a co-parenting team. You have a positive, flexible attitude toward co-parenting, and your child benefits greatly from the friendly post-breakup relationship you and your ex have forged.

You recognize that while consistency is optimal, differences in your respective parenting styles and across the two households are okay. You know that it's good for children to learn that there's more than one way to do things.

You choose your battles wisely. When you and your co-parent do disagree, you model for your child cooperation, problem solving, and healthy coping and conflict-management skills. By your example, your child learns that while life may deal people a hand they don't like or didn't anticipate, healing is possible; peace can emerge from chaos.

Pros

One of the biggest sources of frustration and disappointment for many children in the wake of divorce is that they rarely or never get to be with both parents at the same time anymore. As a child of Super Friends, your child enjoys time with both parents together because the two of you are comfortable being in each other's presence. Writing in the *Daily Beast*, author of *The Anti-Romantic Child: A Memoir of Unexpected Joy* Priscilla Gilman (2012), who endured her own parents' messy divorce, describes her post-breakup parenting partnership:

> We are passionate co-nurturers of and committed co-advocates for our children. We attend every conference together, stand side by side at school events, discuss our children's progress, challenges, triumphs, and setbacks daily. Together we brainstorm cognitive behavioral techniques to help our older son with anxiety and ways to support our

dyslexic son with spelling and reading. As devoted parents of our beloved boys, we are still together, in the words of the Robert Frost poem we printed on our wedding program, "wing to wing, and oar to oar." (n.p.)

Frequent and open communication about your child's welfare sends a message to your child that you are both invested in her well-being. Because their parents are in constant contact, the children of Super Friends are less likely to succeed in playing one parent against the other. They are also less likely to miss opportunities in school or elsewhere, because their parents communicate well about schedules, costs, and other logistics and are willing to be flexible. Super Friends don't waste time squabbling and using the child's activities as a fresh battleground to continue their adult war. They are motivated only by their child's success, not by their personal grievances.

Super Friends help each other parent effectively. Showing respect for your co-parent as a parent and a human being encourages your child to do the same.

Peaceful parenting across two households is a gift that allows your kid to be a kid—free from pressure to demonstrate loyalty to one parent over the other, free to love and enjoy time with both parents without fear, free to connect with a parent's new partner without worrying about upsetting the other parent. By striving to keep tension and conflict to a minimum, you enable your child to thrive even in the face of the emotional upheaval of divorce.

From a parental perspective, being Super Friends means relatively stress-free co-parenting. You don't have to brace yourself or feel dread when your ex's name shows up on your caller ID or in your e-mail inbox.

Cons

You may wonder, *If my child benefits, what could possibly be the downside of this co-parenting style?* Well, there is such a thing as too chummy. Boundaries are important in all relationships, and this one is no exception. If no boundaries are observed, you run the risk of intruding on each other's personal lives and threatening the stability of not only your co-parenting relationship, but also your child's understanding of the permanence of divorce.

Routinely seeing you and your ex interact in super-friendly ways may give your child false hope for reconciliation that goes beyond the usual fantasy about parents getting back together. It's important that you and your ex communicate clearly to your child the permanence of your breakup, while maintaining a cordial yet unmistakably platonic relationship. One co-parenting dad we know so wanted his young daughter to perceive no hostility between him and his ex after the divorce that he would kiss his ex on the lips when greeting her and when saying good-bye. His intention was to reassure his daughter, but such behavior can create confusion for the child, who may wonder: *Is this divorce thing real? Is Daddy moving back with Mommy and me? Will he stay, or will he leave again?*

In the above situation, the child wasn't the only confused party. Dad's new girlfriend was none too pleased, understandably, about the lip-locking. While Super Friends are to be commended for giving their children a stable postdivorce family life, their exceptional co-parenting arrangement might confuse, annoy, or even alienate a new significant other or future mate.

New partners deserve to be shown the respect of clear boundaries between you and your ex. Where these lines are drawn will depend on the individuals involved. In our own co-parenting situation, both of us found new partners who accepted that the two of us vacationed together each summer with our children and shared accommodations in order to save money. We drew the line at sharing a bed. On our website, however, we've heard from new partners who weren't at all happy about such co-parenting family vacations, whether a bed was shared or not. (Now that we have both remarried, we vacation together with our two kids, our respective spouses, Mike's baby daughter, Deesha's stepdaughters, assorted nieces from both families, and far too many canine "children.")

Observing boundaries is necessary to move on from divorce in a healthy way; when new significant others arrive on the scene, their feelings must be factored into this equation as well. Healthy co-parenting relationships include the flexibility to evolve as the circumstances of the people involved in them change.

Super Friends should also be careful not to give their children a distorted sense of reality. No significant human relationship is completely devoid of conflict. While children should not be exposed to high levels of parental conflict, they can learn how to manage the inevitable disagreements that are part and parcel of all relationships by watching you do so.

Finally, don't forget that while you and your ex may get along well and have both come out on the other side of your divorce-related grief, your child may still be struggling. Carolyn Grona (2009), who writes from the perspective of an adult child of divorce at thegrownup-child.ca, says:

> The statement, "Divorce doesn't hurt children, only conflict does" says to me, "Don't worry about helping children with their negative emotions related directly to divorce because there aren't any. Co-parent effectively while conducting yourself appropriately and children of divorce shouldn't have any negative emotions at all." It's an almost ridiculous premise.... Divorce in and of itself, emotionally hurts children....
>
> I understand my parents' divorce. It doesn't make me angry, and I've never once in my whole life wished for them to reconcile. [But my] parents' divorce shattered my core senses of stability, family and love. I was no longer a kid simply worrying about kid things.... My belief in unconditional love came to a screeching halt and I started to wonder what might negate their love for me too. And the fact that my parents never talked badly about one another and never involved me in anything inappropriate didn't help me deal with any of *those* emotions.

In general, Super Friends' ability to get along with each other is highly commendable because of the stability and freedom it affords their children across two households. Just remember that your friendliness isn't all your kids need in order to cope with the divorce and that new partners may feel threatened by it.

Business Partners

As Business Partners, you have fostered an efficient co-parenting relationship that succeeds on the basis of having little extended contact with each other, typically owing to a detailed parenting plan to which you adhere without fail. When conflict does arise, you handle it as you would a professional disagreement—in a cool, detached manner, without burning bridges and without scorching earth.

Because your co-parenting style is driven by your own outlook and behavior, you may be a Business Partner co-parenting with someone who would rather be a Super Friend or someone whose co-parenting style is Oil and Water. In the latter case, your challenge may be to stay above the fray, remembering that while you can't control the other parent, you can control your actions and reactions.

Business Partners sometimes see their children as having two separate lives—one with each parent, never the twain shall meet, and this is how they keep the peace.

Pros

The upside for you is very similar to that for Super Friends—just take away the chumminess and replace it with a businesslike formality. Business Partners generally manage to keep their emotions in check and out of the co-parenting dynamic. Your co-parenting style is often free of overt conflict, so your children are spared the upset that comes with continual exposure to grown-up drama.

With its clear boundaries, the Business Partners relationship makes co-parenting doable for many families. Your kids know without a doubt that you aren't getting back together (though they may still fantasize), and new partners are often more comfortable dating a Business Partner than a Super Friend. Your children's post-divorce reality is a lot like that of Super Friends' kids—again, all the benefits, minus the "Kumbayah" and joint vacations.

Cons

The primary downside of this relationship is that two heads really are better than one. Kids benefit when parents can come together to make decisions on their behalf or even just compare notes about a recent developmental change or school performance issue. "Separate but equal" can leave some important parenting ground uncovered. That's not to say that Business Partners don't ever work together on their children's behalf, but too much laissez-faire can worsen a child's sense of "otherness" after divorce. The child may think, *In "normal" families, parents work together, so if my parents don't work together, we must not be normal—I must not be normal.*

If your children know that your communication with the other parent is minimal, they may take advantage of the situation. "I had no idea that Abby had procrastinated and put off a big school project," said Ali, a co-parenting mom of a sixth-grader. "So when she asked me if she could go out with her friends over the weekend, I said yes because she told me all of her homework was done. So guess who pulled an all-nighter Sunday night. Her father knew about the project, but didn't bother to mention it to me. She's with him most of the time, but he refuses to communicate with me. True, the project was ultimately Abby's responsibility, but having the same information her dad had would have been helpful to me as a parent."

A teen whose parents are Business Partners might also be tempted to tell her mom that she's spending the night at Dad's house when she's really not, banking on the fact that Mom won't call Dad to confirm or check in.

You must also guard against acting passive-aggressively under the guise of a "businesslike" co-parenting approach. Super Friends and

Oil and Water co-parents are very clear about their feelings. Business Partners, on the other hand, present themselves as emotionally neutral. Some really are neutral, while others may be suppressing their anger and grief over the breakup rather than working through their feelings. You owe it to yourself, and to your children, to heal and not hide (refer to chapter 2, "Good Grief: Strategies to Start the Healing Process").

Oil and Water

You and your co-parent just don't mix. The demons from your past intimate relationship—and, possibly, from your ugly divorce proceedings—haunt your current co-parenting efforts. You or your ex (or both of you) may desire sole physical custody of your child, or it may have been awarded to one of you because of alleged parental unfitness or even just because you can't deal with each other. In cases of substantiated unfitness (substance abuse, for example), the fit parent may be stuck in an Oil and Water situation even if she desires a more congenial partnership.

Oil and Water is often the default co-parenting mode for those who struggle to change or to forgive the other for problems during and after the marriage, despite their love for their children.

Pros

By not working in partnership, you and your ex may avoid the awkwardness, strong emotions, and difficult encounters that come with interacting with the other parent. This approach also allows you both to avoid the uncomfortable task of examining your own beliefs and reevaluating your choices and perspective, which is often a necessary step toward cooperative co-parenting.

Yet any "pros" of this approach are benefits only to *you or the other parent personally*, and only in the short term. Parents who are constantly in conflict or who can't function cooperatively on any level are severely limited in their ability to co-parent, to the detriment of their children.

Cons

Shared custody forces Oil and Water co-parents to interact, and all or most of your contact involves bitterness, sniping, dirty looks, the cold shoulder, the silent treatment, all-out shouting matches, or warring e-mails. What should be a simple conversation about summer camp explodes into accusations and lines drawn in the sand. Because you relate this way, opportunities are missed, feelings and boundaries are routinely trampled upon, and nothing is simple. Your child is a witness to it all, explicitly or implicitly drawn into the crossfire. For this reason, Oil and Water is the most damaging of the three co-parenting styles.

Some degree of tension and antagonism between co-parents, especially at the outset of a separation or divorce, is to be expected. There's a time and a place for venting and for letting your anger and frustration rule the day. But that time should have a definite end. For your children's sake, such negativity should not dominate your co-parenting relationship and become a way of life. Oil and Water co-parents often have a lot of unfinished business between them: residual anger, unresolved disagreements, and gripes. Instead of their divorce being an occasion for letting go and a fresh start, Oil and Water co-parents remain entrenched, fighting old battles and licking old wounds. Even if one parent seeks to move forward cooperatively, the other can single-handedly keep the co-parenting relationship mired in dysfunction (though certainly not to the same degree as when both co-parents declare war).

Oil and Water co-parents' never-ending feud creates a heavy burden for their children. The introduction of significant others can exacerbate the situation, making the burden—to show loyalty, to spy, to listen to negative talk—even heavier.

By staying locked in an Oil and Water relationship with your co-parent, you are modeling combativeness and pettiness for your children rather than civility and peacefulness. When you disrespect your co-parent, interfere with his parenting time, and show disdain for his house rules or disciplinary choices, you undermine his authority as a parent and encourage your child toward similar disrespect, or at the very least insecurity and disillusionment.

On top of the pain and loss that come with divorce, children of Oil and Water co-parents are exposed to continued parental disagreements ostensibly centered around them, the children. It's not unusual for children in this situation to think: *What was the point of getting a divorce if they're going to keep fighting with each other? And they're always fighting about me. This is all my fault.* Children of Oil and Water co-parents may experience an exhausting emotional tug-of-war, feeling pressured to "side" with one parent over the other, to love one parent and not the other. Tension between co-parents is confusing and upsetting for children. Already tenuous, their sense of security is threatened every time a new argument erupts. The stress on children of Oil and Water co-parents can lead to emotional and behavioral problems or a decline in school performance.

Not surprisingly, all this conflict isn't good for you as a parent either. It's stressful and tiring to be in a near-constant state of tension, waiting for the next minor misunderstanding to turn into another messy episode in your co-parenting drama. The time and emotional energy you invest in fighting with your ex is time and energy better spent enjoying your child.

The good news is that you can choose to interact differently with your co-parent, starting right now. You can't control your co-parent's behavior, but you can control your own. Make a commitment to turn over a new leaf and extend an olive branch to your ex. If you're not sure how to make a fresh start, or if your ex is unwilling to meet you halfway, refer to the strategies for dealing with a high-conflict co-parent in chapter 12.

As Oil and Water co-parents, you and your ex are ideal candidates for *parallel parenting*, which is a low-conflict alternative to high-conflict co-parenting. Refer to chapter 12 for a detailed discussion about parallel parenting.

Now that you know your co-parenting style and its pros and cons, try the following exercises:

+ Identify one thing you would like to change about how you interact with your ex or how you discuss your ex with your child.

+ Name some changes you can make to improve or strengthen your co-parenting relationship.

+ Ask yourself what you can begin to do *today* to create the kind of co-parenting relationship that will allow your child to look back and say, "My parents broke up, but they worked as a team to take care of me."

Regardless of your co-parenting style, parenting a child across two households is hard work. At the same time, it offers you many opportunities to choose your battles and take the high road. In the next chapter, we'll take a look at some of these opportunities—common co-parenting temptations that require you to be the "bigger" co-parent.

Chapter 5

Fifteen Things You May Want to Do (But Must Not Do) as a Co-parent

To speak ill of your co-parent is to tell your child, "Honey, I love you. But biologically, you are 50% jackass."

—Tara Eisenhard of relativeevolutions.com, a divorce support blog

Perhaps it was the poet and philosopher Sir Charles Barkley who said it most famously: "I am not a role model." In a 1993 Nike commercial soundbite, Barkley articulated his long-held belief that parents should stop looking to him and other athletes to "raise their kids." While a professional basketball player may have the luxury of not worrying about your kids, *you* don't. Like it or not, you and your co-parent are role models for your children, even when you don't feel like acting like role models. The children are always, always watching. And one irony of divorce is that it makes emotional demands of co-parents at precisely the time when their emotional reserves may be at their lowest.

For their children's sake as well as their own, divorced and divorcing parents are called upon to be reasonable, considerate, flexible, cooperative, and mature when what they might really want to do is lash out, compete, be defensive, or dole out some payback—anything to make the pain go away or satisfy the anger burning inside them. But when co-parents are hostile, self-pitying, or passive-aggressive, they send the children the false message that these are appropriate ways to handle conflict and that healing after divorce is not possible.

Instead, children need their co-parents to model healthy ways of coping and dealing with conflict. The following co-parenting "don'ts," while they may be tempting, can ultimately hinder co-parenting success and threaten your child's well-being:

1. Attempt to Sabotage Your Child's Relationship with the Other Parent

As far as your child is concerned, there are no "sides" in your breakup. He needs to have a relationship with both of you, unhindered, without guilt and without concerns about "loyalty" to either of you.

Resist the urge to interfere with your child's time with your ex or to otherwise do or say things to alienate them from each other. Some co-parents intentionally schedule fun outings for their child or sign them up for activities and lessons that conflict with the other parent's parenting time. This forces the child into an emotional tug-of-war, hurting the child as much as, if not more than, the other parent. This can be especially devastating for a child and a nonresidential parent, whose time together is already limited.

Your child's love for and desire to spend time with the other parent is not a rejection of you. Nor should you make your love, affection, and goodwill toward your child conditional upon his rejection of the other parent. Co-parenting is not a zero-sum game.

In fact, trying to undermine your child's relationship with your ex just might backfire. Your child may come to resent you for disrespecting a bond he treasures.

2. Bad-Mouth Your Ex or Your Ex's New Significant Other

Critical, sniping, and mean-spirited words about your ex to or within earshot of your child are wholly inappropriate. Children don't want to hear such things said about their parent—especially by the other parent.

Venomous words about the other parent create conflict within your child because children rightfully identify with *both* parents. So they can't help but wonder what your animosity toward the other parent means for them: *You hate Mommy, but I love Mommy. Does that mean you hate me too? Does that mean I should hate Mommy too? Am I wrong to love Mommy? Do I have to choose to love only one of you?* Don't get your child tied up in these sorts of emotional knots. You're only compounding the sadness, anger, and confusion caused by the breakup. Bad-mouthing your ex may feel good to you in the short run, but the price of the ticket may be long-term harm to your child and to his relationship with both you and your ex.

Even if your ex is failing to hold up her end of the bargain—by not paying child support, skipping her parenting time, or bad-mouthing you—stay above the fray. Be the "bigger" co-parent. Vent to yourself or another adult when your child is not around. Take legal action when advisable. Address and affirm your child's feelings and needs, without confusing them with your own. Comfort your child, instead of sowing seeds of further animosity and negativity.

Let's say your co-parent doesn't follow through on a promise to buy your child shoes for the new school year, and your child is upset. Compare the first response below, which makes unfair generalizations, with the second, which keeps the focus on the child's feelings:

- "I'm so sorry your father let you down again. I knew we couldn't depend on him to get those shoes. He lies about everything!"

- "It sounds as if you're disappointed that Daddy didn't get your new shoes for school like he said he would."

You must insist that family and friends also refrain from bad-mouthing your ex to or around the children. Gripe sessions are okay, perhaps even therapeutic, on occasion—just not around the kids.

It's important that you refrain from negative comments to your children about your ex's new significant other as well; although you may intend such comments to wound someone you may view as your "replacement" or to paint this person in a bad light, you will end up hurting your child and stressing him out. After all, your child has to be in this "bad" person's company, perhaps on a regular basis. And what if your child begins to like this new partner? Allow your child the freedom to get to know the new partner without worries about loyalty to you. Children have plenty of love to go around, and it's not a child's job to make a parent feel better when the parent is feeling threatened or insecure. (We'll talk more about co-parenting and dating in chapter 11.)

Which of the following would be better for your child to hear after a pleasant weekend with your ex and his new girlfriend, Sheila?

- "Sheila is being nice and sweet to you now, but it won't last. She's a home wrecker and gold digger. I know her type."

- "I'm glad you had fun with your dad and Sheila this weekend, honey."

How you feel about Sheila (or Dad, for that matter) is moot. What really matters is your child's peace of mind.

Ugly words may reveal to your child as much, if not more, about you as they do about your ex or his new partner. By bad-mouthing the other parent, you run the risk of damaging your own relationship with your child, showing yourself to be bitter and hostile, and possibly teaching your child bitterness and hostility. More important, investing so much of your energy in negativity will render you incapable of helping your child move forward and heal.

3. Use Your Child as a Messenger

Your ex may well be the last person on the planet you want to talk to or e-mail. But parenting children across two households requires communication between parents. Children shouldn't be burdened with managing the logistics of their daily lives or mediating their parents' exchanges. And frankly, kids aren't always very good messengers. Don't let your parenting partnership become a game of telephone. In subsequent chapters, we'll address different ways to communicate and minimize conflict, but none of these involves sending messages to your ex by way of your children just because you'd rather not talk to her yourself.

We should note, however, that some cooperative co-parents of older children do report relying on their kids to relay minor information. But this is done for practical and logistical reasons, not because the parents want to avoid communicating with each other. In our own family, this seems to be happening naturally as our daughters get older and begin to take more responsibility for their schedules, activities, and possessions. We still communicate face to face and via e-mail, text, and phone, but sometimes we find it convenient to send a message with the kids.

4. Tell Your Child the Grown-Up Details about Why You Broke Up

Understandably, your child will want to know why you're splitting up, and she deserves honest answers. However, she does not want or need to know about Mommy's affair or Daddy's emotional abandonment of the marriage. Adults whose parents divorced when they were kids have told us, without exception, that they did not want to know the intimate details of their parents' split and that they resented the parents who told them anyway.

Your child needs to know only enough to understand two things: (1) what the divorce means for her and (2) that it was not her fault. Beyond practical matters such as your parenting time schedule, it's sufficient to discuss how you and your ex weren't getting along; how you had private, grown-up problems that you couldn't fix; and that you were angry, hurt, and disappointed in each other. Share whatever details apply to your situation *that are also age-appropriate for your child*, in language that she can understand.

It may be that the truth of the matter might be put in one of the following ways:

+ "Over the years, we grew apart and were fighting all the time. Your mother decided to cheat on me, and there was no coming back from that. I tried, but things didn't work out."

+ "The marriage was a mistake from the beginning. We are now finally correcting that mistake."

+ "I don't want this divorce. Your father made this decision. I don't want our family to break up."

But here's what would be appropriate to say to your child:

+ "We've had a lot of grown-up problems that make it very difficult to get along with each other and live together. We worked really hard for a long time to fix these problems, but in the end, we couldn't. For your sake, we wish things could have turned out differently."

+ "It's important for you to know that none of this is your fault. Our love for you is the same and will never change. We've made this decision because of our grown-up problems. We've tried very hard to fix these problems, but we couldn't. For your sake, we wish things could have turned out differently."

If you still aren't sure how much or exactly what to say, try one of the following tactics:

+ Run it by your co-parent first. Chances are, if the two of you can agree on it, it is appropriate to share with your child. Short of having an actual conversation, you could just imagine your ex's reaction if you were to run it by her.

+ Ask yourself, *If I tell my child this, will it likely be a step toward greater peace for the three of us or a step toward further discord?*

+ Ask yourself, *Why am I telling my child this? For the sake of my own interest and needs, or hers?*

5. Try to Convince Your Child That the Divorce Was a Good Idea

Your divorce ended a marriage that you, your ex, or both of you believed was no longer viable. The divorce might have come as a relief to one or both of you, but it created a whole new reality for your child—one he didn't choose and likely doesn't want. A well-meaning parent might try to convince her child that the divorce was a good idea or "for the best," but that's an adult take on the matter. You had every right to get a divorce, and your child has every right not to like it.

Asking children to co-sign on divorce as the best decision for your family is tantamount to asking them to deny their feelings of grief and loss. Even if you believed divorce was the only or the best option, your child may not be able to relate, especially if she was not privy to the adult conflicts that led up to the divorce.

To better honor your child's view of the divorce, follow these three E's:

+ **Explain** to your child that you decided to divorce only after trying really hard to fix your grown-up marital problems.

- **Empathize** with your child. Tell her you understand that your decision has caused her deep pain, but that she can count on you and the other parent to help her adjust and heal.

- But don't try to **enlist** your child's support for the divorce.

Conversely, if you are having your own doubts that the divorce was for the best, or are otherwise struggling to accept it, don't try to get your child's emotional buy-in that the divorce was a mistake. Reach out to a trusted friend or counselor to help you address any ambivalence or regrets you may have.

6. Treat Your Child like a Confidante, Counselor, or Fellow "Victim"

The immediate aftermath of a divorce is rough on everyone involved. It may be easy to lean on your child emotionally because she is sharing parts of this experience along with you, or even simply because she is at hand. But adults should never ask children to shoulder their burdens. Of course you can affirm your child's sadness and disappointment, and share your similar feelings (as appropriate) with her, but be mindful of boundaries in this regard.

Also, if you feel wronged by the divorce itself or the particulars of the proceedings, you may find that you are, wittingly or unwittingly, inviting your child to share in what you perceive as your victimhood. For example, if your ex is balking at your request for support, and your child's tuition is at stake, it may occur to you to discuss with your child the possibility of having to leave school and the unfairness of it all. Or perhaps your divorce settlement mandates the sale of the family home, forcing you to move into a smaller house or an apartment. You may be tempted to tell your child that his other parent is to blame. Don't. This is still a matter that is strictly between the grown-ups. Keep it that way until an agreement has been reached. At that time, if you have to move or your child has to leave private school, it can be discussed appropriately.

The hard reality of divorce is that often people's standards of living do change. Sometimes this is a function of one or both parents' selfishness; other times, there's just not enough money coming in to maintain the same standard of living across two households. Consider the long-term impact of how you choose to discuss matters such as this with your child. Telling her "It's Daddy's fault that you can't go back to private school and we have to move" would be counterproductive. You may feel as though you and your child are the victims of your ex's machinations, but your child may be less inclined than you are to see herself as Daddy's victim.

Co-parents may also confuse their feelings with their children's when they reflect on the problems that plagued the marriage or led to the divorce. Even if you were disappointed by your ex during the course of your marriage, it may be confusing or even frightening for your child to hear things like "Daddy can't be trusted. I hope he doesn't disappoint you." If it turns out that your ex does disappoint your child, then you can help your child deal with this disappointment—while still respecting the ongoing nature of your child's relationship with your ex and not demonizing him.

Your child needs you to be strong enough that she can depend on you for support and understanding, not the other way around. Try not to fall into the self-pity trap, and certainly don't drag your child into it with you. If you are having a hard time holding it together, refer back to chapter 2 for strategies for healing, and seek support from a trusted friend or counselor rather than your child.

7. Major in the Minors

"Making a mountain out of a molehill," "much ado about nothing," "majoring in the minors"...there are countless ways to describe the actions of co-parents who seem to make a hobby of being petty and disagreeable with their ex. While it may be cathartic to give your ex a hard time, remember that by acting this way, you may be indirectly teaching your child to behave that way in her relationships with friends, classmates, and even you. Two unrelated adult children of divorce whom we interviewed for this book both reported childhood memories involving their mothers, their stepmothers, and squabbles over socks—yes, socks—as symbolic of their experience (see the quote at the beginning of chapter 7).

Ignoring your ex's phone calls or e-mails requesting child-related information may give you a sense of control and one-upmanship, but this is false power. Further, your actions (or inactions) are more likely to yield negative consequences for your child than for the intended target of your resistance, your ex.

> Leo, a co-parenting dad of three boys, had 50-50 shared physical and legal custody of his children. His youngest son wanted to play soccer, and in order to sign him up, Leo needed to have his ex on board because some practices and games took place during her parenting time. Previously, Leo's ex had expressed resentment that Leo enrolled their kids in activities and took them on outings that she couldn't afford to join them on. Leo had no problem assuming the full cost of the activities, but his ex accused him of trying to make her "look bad" because of her inability to pay. So she began to ignore Leo's e-mails and phone calls related to extracurricular activities for their children. As a result, Leo could not enroll the boys in any activities that occurred during her parenting time, including soccer. Understandably, the children were disappointed. Ultimately, Leo had to take the matter to family court, where a parenting plan was drafted that stipulated that the children would be allowed to participate in extracurricular activities, supported by both parents.

Like many co-parents who remain resentful toward their exes, Leo's ex hadn't worked through her anger. For some suggestions on more productive responses to anger, refer back to the "Journaling through the Grief Process" section in chapter 2. If you're struggling with anger because you aren't able to forgive your ex, see chapter 6 (specifically number 14) for a discussion about how forgiveness can be freeing for you as well as for your ex.

Let your child see you controlling your anger, choosing your battles, and working civilly with your co-parent to mind the details of her care and well-being. Let her see you not sweating the small stuff. And when you and your ex do disagree, let your child see you managing conflict respectfully and maturely. In these ways, you are modeling discernment, teamwork, appropriate compromise, and cooperation. You are also letting your child know that she's so important that both of you are committed to working together for her good.

8. Use Your Child as a Weapon to Wound Your Ex

Picture the following scene.

> Your ex is four months behind on child support, *and* you don't like her new significant other. *I'll show her,* you think. You fire off an e-mail telling her not to bother picking the kids up for her week with them. Until she pays up and stops exposing the kids to that low-life slacker boyfriend of hers, she's not allowed to see them.

You don't want this to be the beginning of an episode in your co-parenting life, because it will likely end in one of three ways:

Scenario 1. Your ex shows up anyway, and the two of you have an ugly fight in front of the kids. And possibly the neighbors. Worse, she brings her slacker boyfriend with her, which only escalates the conflict. Worse still, she brings the cops with her. While police officers generally don't intervene in such matters once they establish that a child is not in danger—choosing instead to refer co-parents back to family court to settle their differences—their mere presence may frighten and upset your children.

Scenario 2. Your ex doesn't show up. Your kids are upset, disappointed, and confused. What little stability and security you've been able to establish in their lives since the divorce is now shattered. They were used to the routine of the parenting time schedule, but now you've pulled the rug from under them. Changes in the schedule shouldn't happen suddenly, on an angry whim, and without adequate support for the children, including counseling if need be.

Scenario 3. Your ex doesn't show up at your place, but she does get a judge to hold you in contempt for violating the court-ordered terms of your parenting plan. Not only is the slacker boyfriend still in the picture, there's still no guarantee of child support…and you've had to take time off from work to go to court.

Regardless of the scenario, the bottom line is that you've upset your children and further alienated the one person in the world who is supposed to be your primary partner in this parenting gig. It's just not worth it.

Generally speaking, parenting time is a separate issue from child support, in the eyes of the court. Child support is not the "admission price" your ex pays you to see the children. Unless your ex's parental rights have been terminated, those rights include parenting time. She does not automatically forfeit these rights because she failed to pay child support (or has bad taste in men). The same system that can work for you to recover the unpaid child support can also work on your ex's behalf if you do not honor the court-mandated parenting time schedule.

Here's how you can rewrite the script—this time with a parentally responsible, if not happy, ending:

First, look in the mirror: honestly consider which of your complaints about the boyfriend are your opinion or conjecture, which are born of your discomfort with having someone you don't know around your children, and which actually involve potential harm to your children. Share your legitimate concerns about the boyfriend (and about the late child support) with your ex, in writing if need be. Invite her response. Send your children off at the regular pick-up time with a hug and a smile.

Then, if your ex continues to remain in arrears, contact your local child support enforcement office for assistance with the delinquent payments. Take legal action if you still have concerns about your children's safety or well-being or if you believe they are in need of counseling and your ex is against it. A court-approved parenting plan may help address any unresolved issues.

9. Punish Grandma and Grandpa

Sometimes grandparents, along with their grandchildren, are casualties in the war between the exes. Children lose so much in the wake of divorce or separation; cherished relationships with their grandparents should not be among those losses. In fact, as long as grandparents don't add to the conflict and confusion, they can be a source of much-needed comfort to their grandchildren, to their adult child, and perhaps even to their former daughter- or son-in-law.

In her "10 Commandments of Co-Parenting," Lynn Nelson (1995, n.p.), a co-parent and public relations specialist, observes: "Your in-laws are probably as disappointed as you and your former partner about the dissolution of your relationship. Grandparents can be a child's greatest cheerleaders; don't hurt your children and yourself by cutting off visits with them. In many cases, grandparents also provide back-up child care; this isn't something any single parent should give up willingly."

One of the greatest gifts that Mike's parents have given Deesha is their continued love, care, and friendship. And for our daughters, Grandma and Grandpa's house is their third home—a safe, loving, and neutral ground.

10. Get Rid of Family Photos and Other Keepsakes

A lot of cleaning house takes place in the aftermath of divorce, literally and figuratively. (We even advised this in chapter 2.) Wedding and other photos that include your co-parent may be among the first things in the "get rid of" pile, and understandably so. Those pictures can serve as painful reminders of what was, and they can trigger feelings of regret, hurt, anger, and disappointment. But before you haul out the shredder, consider this: Those aren't just your memories. They are part of your children's memories as well, memories of their pre-divorce family history.

One of co-parenting's most important tenets and biggest challenges is seeing your ex and the divorce through your child's eyes. To your child, those pictures are still treasures, perhaps even more cherished now that the family he once knew is no more. With divorce, you are not able to give your child the intact family he desires, but you can allow him to hold on to memories and symbols of what was, even if *you* don't want to hold on to them.

This is not to say that you should keep your 14-by-17-inch wedding portrait hanging over the fireplace. Perhaps this portrait or a smaller one can be hung in your child's room or placed on his nightstand. The photos that are painful for you to see can be compiled into a photo album for him to keep in a special place to look through whenever he wants.

Some parents worry that keeping family photos will feed their children's fantasy of a parental reconciliation that's never going to happen. They don't want to encourage such fantasies because they don't want to add to the children's disappointment. But the reality for many kids is no matter how much evidence to the contrary, no matter how many photos you take away, they will hold on to that fantasy. M. Gary Neuman, LMHC, author of *Helping Your Kids Cope with Divorce the Sandcastles Way* (1998), cautions parents against underestimating the power of the reunion fantasy. Neuman, whose divorce therapy program for children is mandated in family court by several states, notes that a child's identity is tied to his family's identity. So the break-up of the family as the child has known it threatens the child's sense of self, even if he remains close to both parents. For this reason, many children persist in believing that their parents will reconcile even after one or both parents remarry; a healthy sense of self is at stake (Abel, n.d.). It's important to talk to your children about the permanence of divorce, but it's also important to respect the pre-divorce keepsakes and memories they treasure. Further, destroying the photos may suggest to your child that her family is being destroyed. This does not have to be the case. Allowing your child to keep treasured photos can affirm to her that even though her family is made up of two separate households, with parents who lead separate lives, she is still part of a loving, caring family.

11. Rush into Another Relationship or Expose Your Child to the Revolving Door of Your Dating Life

Quickly finding another partner or jumping headfirst into the dating scene might be tempting for you as a newly separated or divorced parent, especially if your ex has already moved on to someone else. Loneliness, fear, regret, vulnerability, the desire to "make up for lost time," or the desire to show your ex (and everyone else) how easily you've moved on can lead to your rushing into a new relationship before the wounds from the previous one have had a chance to heal.

Instead of trying to use another person to dull the pain or quell the jealousy, face your post-breakup struggles head-on. The last thing you want to have to deal with (or worse, for your child to have to deal with, directly or indirectly) is the trauma of *another* breakup on the heels of the first one. If you are having a hard time adjusting to being single, revisit chapter 2 for some strategies.

As a parent, you are charged with protecting your child physically and emotionally. Even if you wait until you've begun to heal before dipping your toe into the dating pool again, it's not a good idea to introduce your child to everyone you date. In addition to considering safety issues, you must also use discretion when allowing your children to get attached to other adults in the wake of your breakup. The dating life is uncertain, filled with ups and downs; your children should be spared the roller-coaster ride.

It's fine for your child to know, when the time is right, that you are dating. But sharing the specifics of whom you're dating and to what extent, and having your child meet this person, should be undertaken only after much time and consideration. (How much time? We'll talk about that in chapter 11.)

Let your child see you being selective about whom you choose to introduce her to and in what capacity. By doing so, you are modeling prudence, patience, and good judgment. You're also letting her know that, as one mom put it, "only friends who are special enough get to meet her, because she's just that special to me."

12. Pressure Your Child to Approve of Your New Relationship

Just because you're done mourning your old relationship doesn't mean that your child is, nor that she should be. It's unfair to expect a child to give Mommy's new relationship her stamp of approval when she is still mourning Mommy and Daddy's old relationship. Don't make acceptance of your new partner a hoop through which your child must jump to prove her loyalty or to make you happy. Your happiness is not your child's responsibility.

Give your child the time, space, and support she needs to work through the mix of feelings—curiosity, excitement, resentment, sadness, and ambivalence—she may feel once she's aware that you're involved with someone else.

Also, don't assume that your child's reluctance to embrace this new person is your ex's fault. But do acknowledge that your child may be struggling with questions of loyalty to the other parent now that you've introduced a potential stepparent. Help her address these feelings and concerns.

Take your time and enjoy your new relationship. And be sure to give your child permission to make her own peace with it.

13. Buy Things for Your Child out of Guilt or to Compete with Your Ex

When we asked the members of our CoParenting101.org Facebook group about indulging their children after the divorce, they responded with all sorts of examples, from "divorce-guilt dogs" (and one "divorce-guilt cat") to ice cream and other treats. "That first Christmas morning postdivorce?" said Mary, mom of a teenage son, "My living room looked like Toys 'R' Us." Mary succumbed to what is commonly known as "divorce guilt"—guilt about spending less time with the kids or about the divorce in general.

"I wanted to make it up to my kids," said Brad, a father of three, "so I bought them a puppy. Well, by the next Christmas that puppy was a sad, lonely dog that no one cared about but me. And I still felt guilty about the divorce."

"They cried; I purchased," said Ilana, who has a son and a daughter. "But six years later, I'm over it."

In addition to divorce guilt, there are other reasons co-parents may fall into a spending trap: buying things to make themselves or the kids feel better; uncertainty as to how to relate to and connect with their children; or "making up for lost time" if their spending was limited during the marriage. Add one or more of these scenarios to a contentious co-parenting situation, and a parent may be tempted to "buy" a child's affections, loyalty, or cooperation.

A well-timed trip to Disney World, a new car for a teenager, or expensive toys can tip the scales in the buying parent's favor if a child is allowed to have input into her living arrangements and the parenting time schedule. Family court judges tend to frown upon one parent's attempts to outspend the other in order to curry a child's favor, especially in the midst of a custody dispute. Do all you can to avoid the appearance of this.

Even when custody is not at stake, a child can be essentially bribed into favoring one parent over the other or wanting to spend less time with the parent who doesn't indulge him. In such cases, the fault lies not with the child for accepting the gifts, but with the co-parent who would use such tactics. The message the child receives is that the value of a relationship is based on the amount of material things you get out of it, not the love and care shared between the people in the relationship. The child learns to regard her parents and others primarily based on what they can give her and do for her.

Jillian, a mom of three, made a conscious effort not to compete with her ex when it came to spending. "It was really important to me that they didn't get spoiled through the divorce. I focus on what they need, not on what they want. And in the process, they're learning the difference between needs and wants."

While one parent may legitimately have more resources or disposable income and may spend more money on the children, the problem comes when this distinction is used to manipulate a child or compete with the other parent. Always give yourself a time-out if you're thinking of ways to diminish your ex in your child's eyes.

If you feel tempted to spend money on your child to assuage your guilt or to compete with the other parent, try this instead: spend time with your child doing something that requires little or no money. Children crave parental time and attention more than anything else, especially during and in the wake of a divorce.

14. Bash Marriage, Relationships, or Your Ex's Gender

Some individuals emerge from the rubble of a broken relationship with strong anti-marriage, anti-commitment, misogynist (woman-hating), or misanthropist (man-hating) sentiments. They apply their traumatic personal experiences to all of humanity. That's unfortunate, but it's fairly innocuous for the adults in their lives, who can just let their calls go to voicemail or otherwise choose not to listen to their diatribes. But for their children, it's confusing and unsettling to hear a parent rant and rail against the very institution into which they were born and that they may wish to pursue later in life.

Neither sons nor daughters should hear Dad, for example, making ugly or sweeping generalizations about women, particularly during the preteen and teen years when they are sorting out desires and attractions and trying to make sense of cultural messages about what it means to be a man or a woman.

Similarly, children should not be told that all men are [insert your negative stereotype here] or hear their father referred to as a "deadbeat dad," regardless of his shortcomings.

15. Wallow

"I will never forgive your mother for what she did to us!" "I'll never forgive your grandmother for taking your father's side!" If your child sees you endlessly and deeply mired in the disappointments, hurts, and betrayals that contributed to your breakup, you are not modeling the strategies he needs to cope with and eventually thrive in the aftermath of your breakup.

You are also, perhaps unintentionally, putting pressure on your child such that he is afraid to make a mistake or otherwise cross you. You are sending the message that if he does something that you don't like, you might write him off forever too.

If instead your child sees you healing, forgiving, and moving past the problems that contributed to your breakup, you are modeling strength, grace, and resilience. Instead of hosting pity parties and burning bridges, model effective problem-solving and resolve conflicts. Model hope!

We hope the above list can be a blueprint for your cooperative co-parenting relationship and give you some stepping-stones to help your child thrive after divorce. If you're lamenting that you've already done some of these "don'ts," you're not alone; only a saint would be able to completely avoid these very common responses to divorce and co-parenting. Even though you love your children and want what's best for them, it's not always easy to do the right thing. And some days are tougher than others. But each day is a new opportunity to be a good role model.

So...what will you model for your child today?

Chapter 6

Fifteen Things You Must Do (But May Not Want to Do) as a Co-parent

Divorce is hard. Co-parenting is even harder.

—Maria, co-parenting mom of a high school-age son

A co-parent's work is never done. Not only must you *avoid* the mine-field of negative behaviors that can undermine your parenting part-nership, but it's in your children's best interest for you to *adopt* civil and conciliatory behaviors as well. The following action-oriented guidelines make cooperative kid-centered parenting across two households possible.

1. Know Which Pitches to Swing At and Which to Let Pass

Like a lot of siblings, our daughters, Taylor and Peyton, have a knack for getting under each other's skin, so we often tell them, "Don't swing at everything that's pitched." We want our kids to learn to take some things in stride and to recognize that not everything their sister or their peers say warrants a response. This is also true for co-parents. "When my boy tells stories about me he heard from his dad," said Kelly, a mom of two, "I think about driving down a very low road. Then I breathe, blink twice, and move on."

Disagreements, misunderstandings, and conflict are inevitable, even when both co-parents are committed to being cooperative. Knowing which pitches to swing at—and which to let pass—is the key to your peace of mind as a co-parent. Consider:

What can you let go? Short of harm to your child, you don't have a say as to what happens at your ex's house during her parenting time. If it's a matter of different parenting styles, let it go. If, for example, you think your child doesn't eat healthy food at your ex's house, you can discuss your concerns with your ex and try to get on the same page, but you should recognize that ultimately, it's his house, his time, his choices. You can't control what he feeds your child during his parenting time, but you can make sure your child eats healthy, balanced meals when she's with you.

Stay laser-focused on your child's needs, and let everything else go. Disengage strategically—don't give your co-parent the silent treatment or ignore conflict, but avoid playing tit for tat or going on the defensive. Ignore any negative communication from your ex that's not specifically about your child. Walk away, or hang up the phone, if tensions begin to escalate or if your ex is arguing just to get a rise out of you or for attention (it happens).

Not swinging at your ex's pitches is not the same as being a doormat. You are very powerfully asserting to your co-parent your boundaries and that your priority is your child's well-being. As far as what they can and what they can't let go, different co-parents draw the line in different places. And where you draw the line at the outset of your breakup may be different from where you draw it a year later as, hopefully, by that time you and your co-parent have settled into a groove, respecting each other's boundaries and minimizing the conflict.

And when a "swing" is warranted? Here are some suggestions on how to avoid striking out:

+ **Respond; don't react.** Short of life-threatening emergencies, few e-mails and phone calls require an immediate response. Sleep on the matter and respond when, hopefully, you and your ex are calmer. If you're the one initiating a potentially volatile exchange, think before you speak (or type), and choose your words carefully. Maintain a businesslike tone, and keep your message brief and child-focused.

+ **Ask questions and use "I" statements, instead of leading with demands, accusations, or ultimatums.** You're more likely to defuse a heated situation with "I'm concerned about Lisa's grades too, and I would be happy to talk with you about how we can help her get back on track" than with "You have a lot of nerve calling *me* irresponsible! *You're* the one who doesn't check her homework!" even if the latter is true.

+ **Listen.** New York–based mediator Gene A. Johnson Jr. once tweeted this advice: "Particularly in the beginning of a conflict, keep an open mind and a closed mouth" (@geneajohnsonjr, Mar. 20, 2010, 12:00 p.m.).

+ **Take a problem-solving approach.** Sift through all the angry grown-up stuff that's swirling around, and get to the child-related problem. Then attack the *problem*, not your ex. For one example of this approach, see the heading "Filter Your Ex's Communications" in chapter 12.

2. Be the "Bigger" Co-Parent

Even when you're not swinging at everything your ex pitches, it's still possible to get burned out on co-parenting, especially when your co-parent isn't pulling his weight. When that happens, your child needs you to be the "bigger" co-parent. Being the "bigger" co-parent means doing the right thing for your child regardless of what your co-parent does or doesn't do. See also *turning the other cheek, not fighting fire with fire, holding your tongue,* and any number of other idioms for *don't sink to his level.* Easier said than done, right? Here's what some "bigger" co-parents we interviewed had to say:

- "Oh, the things *I* could tell the kids about *him*...but I don't. Yet he bad-mouths me to them every chance he gets."

- "Their dad disappoints them constantly, but the heavens open up when he just barely comes through...with crumbs. I'm tired of the fact that he can do so little, tell so many lies, and still be the hero."

- "It would be nice if she helped out with transportation. But running kids back and forth is beneath her. When the kids are sick, I take off work and get them to the hospital or doctor. The oldest has severe asthma, so we're at the hospital at least once a month. When it came time for the puberty talk, I'm the one that handled that. Birthday parties and vacations? I plan. School functions? I volunteer. School clothes and shoes? I buy. Teacher conferences? I handle it. And yet in the blink of an eye, [in the kids' eyes] I am in the back of the line."

- "Being the bigger parent is exhausting and sometimes you just friggin' *lose it...*"

Can you relate? Maybe parenting feels like a thankless job as you sacrifice (gladly) for your children, but still it chafes a little— sometimes more than a little—when your co-parent neglects your children's emotional or material needs. Yet you don't begrudge your kids the right to love their parents unconditionally. Still…you're tired of bearing the load alone. And tired of fighting. So you stop fighting, but continue to bear the weight of your children's pain, confusion, and disappointment, and the primary responsibility for their care, despite a shared parenting agreement. There's only so much family court can do. Thoughts of some kind of comeuppance for your ex are quickly shot down. "My child is a human shield," one frustrated co-parenting dad told us. "There's nothing I can do to put a stop to what my ex is doing that won't hurt my kid in some way." You want to do what's right, but quietly seethe at the fact that you're the only parent willing to cease fire for your children's sake. You want to be the "bigger" co-parent, to take the high road. But the high road feels like a high-wire act: how to balance your sanity, your kids' best interest, and your frustration?

Taking the focus off his ex was the strategy Ray used. "I worked on improving myself. That, combined with perseverance and prayer, has resulted in a better co-parenting partnership. My ex brings the fuel and I refuse to light the match."

Linda, a co-parenting mom, found Rodin's words to be true: "Patience is also a form of action" (www.quotegarden.com/patience.html). Linda told us, "Over time, I let [my ex] reveal himself to my boy, and the pain was honest and unencumbered by my input. Sometimes you have to love enough to be there [for your child], strong and able to pick up the shards, with just the right touch of support."

Sophia, who describes her ex and his wife's behavior toward her as "belligerent," shared how "standing down" helped her children:

> It's been awful at times to bite my tongue and "stand down" while trying to work things out for my kids with their dad and his wife. I try to do everything in the kids' best interest, but I almost always feel like it's a losing battle, and I'm hitting my head up against a wall.
>
> I've always just kept quiet, tried to make peace, not fought back. Often, my own friends and family wanted me to show some anger, demand justice, hit them between the eyes with what I know are my rights as a parent. But the

path I've chosen is to simply do what I know to be best for my kids, which often meant looking the other way, turning the other cheek, and not responding to the other parent's ridiculous attempts to arm-wrestle every little thing.

I've done it for nine years now, and I can honestly tell you, it pays off in the end. My kids are eleven, thirteen, and seventeen now, and they see for themselves how difficult their dad and stepmom have made things unnecessarily, and how I have always protected them, shielded them, ultimately, by standing down from the tug-of-war that could have ensued.

It takes two to fight. If you just step back, let go, do the right thing no matter what, your kids will have a better chance to escape becoming a casualty of divorce. Mine have.

I know it's the hardest thing to do sometimes, but it's what's best for them in the long run. You are being the better parent for it, even though for many years, you will probably be the unsung hero.

Here are some suggestions for communicating with your ex—things you can say—when you need to be the "bigger" co-parent:

- "I'm hanging up the phone now. I can't talk to you when you use disrespectful language. When you can speak to me respectfully and keep the focus on what's best for our child, I'll be happy to take your call."

- "I believe if we can keep the focus on our child, and not our feelings about each other, we can solve this problem and help our child."

- "I understand that you're angry about the decision I made. But we'll need to end this conversation until you can speak to me without yelling."

- "Because our conversations often end up in shouting matches, I will be communicating with you via e-mail, except in cases of emergency related to our child."

* "Your personal feelings about my significant other are not the issue. Let's keep the focus on our child's needs."

It's okay if you sound like a broken record. The message really is the same regardless of the specifics of the situation: "Let's stay focused on what's in the best interest of our child."

3. Take Responsibility

When your children witness you at a less-than-proud co-parenting moment (it happens to all co-parents), let them also see you not blame the other parent for it ("Your mother makes me so angry! I wouldn't have said that if she hadn't…"), instead taking full responsibility for your actions. You can't control other people, but you can control yourself.

4. Be Flexible

Parenting plans, which we'll discuss in detail in chapter 8, are great for helping minimize conflict between co-parents. These agreements delineate the parenting time schedule—including holidays—and many other practical matters related to parenting across two households. But then, life happens…work schedules change, special events or vacation opportunities arise that don't match the schedule, and sometimes paternal Grandma's seventieth birthday celebration falls during Mom's parenting time.

While kids do thrive on the consistency and stability a schedule provides, there are times when a little flexibility can go a long way in the best interest of your kids. Usually, if you weigh the pros (the kids get to go on a special trip, event, or outing) and the cons (the kids will be with *him* during *my* time), you'll find that your flexibility is worth it because your kids are worth it.

When co-parents are willing to swap days or give up some of their parenting time to the other parent, kids get to enjoy special times and make memories. They also get to see their parents cooperating and being considerate of each other and of them. Finally, they get the message that while the schedule does matter, *they* matter most.

5. Lose the Sense of Entitlement

A common roadblock to cooperative co-parenting occurs when one parent feels entitled to more parenting time than the other or believes the other isn't entitled to *any* parenting time. The entitled parent considers himself the *real* parent or the better parent. He wants the other parent to go away, or he tries to act as a gatekeeper to the child. The lesson this parent needs to learn was taught in kindergarten: share.

You may believe your ex's infidelity or character flaws render her undeserving of time and closeness with your child, but your child deserves and has a right to this relationship, regardless. If you can do more than just grudgingly accept that your child has a relationship with the other parent, your child will benefit greatly.

6. Enjoy Your Child-Free Time

Consider it a glass-half-full approach to co-parenting: though you miss your child when she is with the other parent, your co-parenting arrangement affords you child-free time that's yours for the taking. Some parents we know spend their kid-free time salsa dancing, running home businesses, writing, cleaning and de-cluttering, taking martial arts classes, attending book clubs, eating out at nice restaurants, traveling, dating, or sleeping in.

Some co-parents struggle with deep sadness when their children are with the other parent, even in the absence of safety concerns. They feel as if they are missing out on parts of their children's childhoods, or they believe this aspect of their divorce is unfair, particularly if they didn't want the divorce. We encourage them to acknowledge and work through those feelings and also to see the situation through their children's eyes. Shared custody allows their children to enjoy time with both parents.

If missing your kids has kept you from enjoying your child-free time, try to find comfort in the fact that, despite the divorce, your kids are having moments of joy—even if you're not present for all of them.

7. Respect Your Child's Relationship with the Other Parent

Regardless of what happened in your marriage or since the breakup, your child has a right to have a relationship with both parents if both are fit and willing, without micromanagement or interference from the other parent. Divorce brings a lot of change and uncertainty for children, but having a relationship with both parents is one thing they should be able to count on, enjoy, and not feel conflicted about.

Try to be a gateway, not a gatekeeper. When the other parent and your child communicate by phone or e-mail, refrain from monitoring, discouraging contact, or cutting their time short. Also, be flexible with the parenting time schedule when possible, and let your child know that you're happy that she's happy when she spends time with the other parent. Instead of negative comments, silence, or eye-rolling (some parenting plans specifically forbid this!) when your child tells you about her time with the other parent or expresses a desire to see the other parent, be positive and interested. If need be, gently ask questions (without prying) to convey to your child that it's okay to share with you her experiences with the other parent and that you know how special this relationship is to her. This will go a long way in letting her know that she's free to love both parents openly.

8. Encourage Your Child to Respect the Other Parent

The best way to encourage your child to respect the other parent is to demonstrate that respect yourself. Respect does not equal agreement; you may disagree with your ex's parenting style, her religious beliefs and practices, whom she dates, and other choices, but short of any harm coming to your child, you can still show respect for or at least hold your tongue about them.

Remember also to respect the fact that the relationship your ex has with your child is a *parenting* relationship. Unconditionally, your ex is entitled to the same respect from your child that you expect as a parent. Recognize that during his parenting time, it's his house, his rules, his way. It's normal for kids, especially teens, to chafe at authority and try to push the boundaries of their independence. But it's not appropriate for one parent to encourage or support disrespect toward the other parent. Suggesting to your child that she doesn't have to listen to Daddy or follow his rules is a recipe for needless confusion, disruption, and drama.

9. Keep the Lines of Communication Open

Keeping each other up-to-date on your child's social, emotional, physical, and educational well-being at all times is essential to your child's healthy growth and development. But for some co-parents, the anger and the pain related to the breakup is so present that any interaction with their ex is upsetting or enraging. To avoid the emotional upheaval or to punish the other parent, these parents cut off communication with their ex. (See our discussion of Oil and Water co-parents in chapter 4.)

Co-parenting isn't possible without some level of communication. Using children as messengers isn't an option, so co-parents must be willing to stay in touch and share information. If face-to-face and telephone communication proves too volatile, some co-parents use e-mail or texting. But remember that with e-mail and texting you don't have the benefit of tone of voice, facial expression, or other non-verbal clues to soften words that might otherwise sound harsh. Allow for possible misunderstandings of tone and intentions, and ask for clarification before responding.

10. See Your Ex through Your Child's Eyes

If negative feelings about your child's other parent just won't subside, try seeing him through your child's eyes. A child looks at a parent, warts and all, with love. You may no longer share these feelings, but the other parent remains central to your child's life and well-being. So when you interact with your ex, do so as you would with any person who is important to your child—with respect and civility.

11. Mind Your Business

It's unfortunate, but some co-parents attempt to use their children to spy on the other parent. Anything that happens in your ex's personal life or during her parenting time that doesn't harm your kids is no longer your concern. If you do believe something is going on that is harmful or potentially harmful, communicate your concerns to your ex, acknowledging her right to privacy, right to discipline, and right to make decisions regarding your child's welfare, including health, education, and religion, if you share legal custody. (For more about legal versus shared custody, see chapter 7).

Angelique, a co-parenting mom of one, uses this rule of thumb: "If the issue is not something I'd call child protective services about if it were happening at my neighbor's house, I stay out of it."

12. Move On

Simply put, though not simple to do: let go of the old relationship. Doing so frees you to be a fully engaged parent and a more cooperative co-parent.

13. Turn Over a New Leaf

Each day, each interaction, is an opportunity to repair and rebuild a damaged co-parenting relationship. How you started is not how you're destined to end. Be willing to extend (and accept) olive branches, for your child's sake.

14. Offer (or Ask for) Forgiveness

Many of the dos and don'ts we're sharing may sound impossible given the intense feelings and fallout many co-parents experience in the wake of a breakup. What helped us and other co-parents get to a place where we could focus primarily on our children (and not each other) was a clear separation between our past marital relationship and our current parenting partnership. We consider our old relationship dead and buried. When unresolved issues from this relationship "rise from the dead," we think of them as zombies that can terrorize our parenting partnership, as we suggested in chapter 2. That's pretty dramatic imagery, but some co-parents have found it helps them envision what's stopping them from moving forward as a team.

One thing that can help keep the walking dead of your old relationship at bay is forgiveness. Here are two quotes related to forgiveness that we think are especially applicable to co-parenting:

Forgiveness doesn't make the other person right. It sets you free.

—Becca, co-parenting mom of three

Resentment is like taking poison and hoping the other person dies.

—Saint Augustine

We've repeated the Saint Augustine quote from chapter 2 here because resentment is the reason many co-parents refuse to forgive their exes. This refusal not only prevents them from building a strong parenting partnership, but also keeps them and their children needlessly burdened by the past.

Sometimes forgiveness is a gift given in words, but it doesn't have to be. You can choose to forgive your former spouse inwardly, in your heart. You can also ask your ex or your children for forgiveness—even if forgiveness is not granted, the apology alone can be freeing for you.

Remember also that when you forgive, you are modeling forgiveness for your child.

Perhaps the person you need to forgive is yourself—for matters related to your marriage, your divorce, or your co-parenting situation to date. This may also be a crucial step toward healing and putting your old relationship to rest. You can't go back and change who you were and what you did in your marriage, but you can forgive yourself, be kind to yourself, and build the next chapter of your life to reflect the lessons you've learned.

15. Look to the Future

Your child won't be a child forever. If you're wrangling with the other parent right now over issues related to your child, these may no longer be issues when your young child becomes a teen or when your teen becomes an adult. But adulthood isn't necessarily the end of your connection to your ex, if you factor in higher education and possibly weddings and grandchildren. Will your present co-parenting conflicts even matter then? Do they really matter now, in the grand scheme of things?

In ten or twenty years, what do you want your kids to say about their childhood and how *you* co-parented? What will your child have learned about managing conflict and relationships from watching you as a co-parent? What changes can you make with regard to how you engage your co-parent so that your child can look back fondly on this chapter of her life?

Even if your ex is less than civil, your efforts to be a peaceful and cooperative co-parent are a loving investment in your child's present and future well-being. The next chapter explores what this investment looks like from a logistical standpoint: the practical and day-to-day basics of parenting across two households.

Chapter 7

Calendars, Clothes, and Camps

There's something my dad still refers to as the "sock wars" that was mostly between my mom and ex-stepmother. My mom would write lists of clothing that I brought to my dad's house on the weekends so that I wouldn't forget to bring them back home, which seems logical to me. My stepmother would find the lists and start complaining about them because she thought I should feel at home there and be able to leave clothing there, which now also seems logical to me.

—Mark, adult child of divorce

When it comes to divorce, the oft-asked question "What about the children?" can take on multiple meanings. One of these has to do with the children's emotional well-being, while another focuses on practical and logistical matters related to co-parenting and is the subject of this chapter.

The most basic co-parenting consideration is the parenting time schedule: when will the children live with one parent, and when will they live with the other? Other details must be worked out as well: What time will the children be picked up during transitions? Or will they be dropped off instead? What will you do if there is a scheduling conflict? With whom will the kids spend the holidays? Who should be responsible for buying—and laundering—the kids' clothes? Who pays for camps, other extracurricular activities, and unexpected expenses? Which parent can claim the children for tax purposes? Who will take off work when one of the kids is sick or has a routine medical or dental appointment? Will you do parent-teacher conferences separately or jointly? What happens if you or your co-parent relocates outside of your current school district? What if one of you currently lives or later moves out of state?

For some co-parents, dealing with these necessary tasks and decisions can easily become a fresh battleground for old conflicts from their marriage. However, by planning ahead and agreeing on the particulars of these matters, co-parents can minimize future conflict. Unfortunately, however, of the e-mails we receive from co-parents and partners of co-parents (usually girlfriends) seeking advice, about half involve high-conflict situations where there is no parenting plan on file with the court. Over and over again, these parents find themselves embroiled in arguments as they struggle with co-parenting basics that are typically covered in parenting plans. We'll guide you through writing your own parenting plan in the next chapter. But first, we'll lay out the core issues that you and your co-parent will likely need to discuss and negotiate in order to finalize a plan for co-parenting your child.

How Will You Share Parenting Time?

A fundamental question children have about divorce is "Who will I live with now?" The answers co-parents come up with vary, but should reflect a child's best interest and his right to continue to have a relationship and spend time with both parents. For this reason, parenting time should not be withheld or limited to retaliate against a parent for seeking a divorce, for the outcome of the divorce settlement, or for problems in the marriage. Nor should parenting time be viewed as a reward for paying child support, one that can be taken away if a parent falls into arrears. There *are* penalties for failure to pay child support, but loss of parenting time is not one of them.

Knowing what to expect because there's a schedule in place can give children and adults a measure of comfort, stability, and security in the midst of the upheaval and uncertainty of separation and divorce. The schedule you choose will depend in part on the type of custody arrangement you have.

First, Some Legal Lingo

We have been intentional in this book about using the phrase "parenting time," not "visitation," to describe the time that a child spends with a parent. Letting a child know that she has two homes and is not a visitor in either of them goes a long way toward helping her understand that she is still a part of a loving family, with two devoted parents. Legally speaking, however, things aren't so simple. There are two types of custody: physical custody and legal custody.

Physical custody means responsibility for the daily and immediate physical care and supervision of the child.

+ A parent who has **sole** (also referred to as **primary**) **physical custody** is primarily responsible for the daily supervision of the child and for her immediate physical care. This is the parent with whom the child lives for most of the year. Unless the other parent, the **noncustodial** (or **nonresidential**) parent, is determined unfit by the court or chooses to relinquish her parental rights, she retains rights to parenting time (sometimes referred to as visitation).

+ **Shared physical custody** is an arrangement in which parents who live apart share responsibility for the daily supervision of the child and for her immediate physical care, based on a set schedule.

Legal custody means responsibility for making important decisions about the child's welfare, such as educational, legal, religious, and major medical decisions.

+ A parent who has sole legal custody is responsible for making educational, legal, religious, and major medical decisions for the child. Unless a judge rules otherwise, the custodial parent must keep the noncustodial parent advised of the child's status with regard to health, education (for example, grades), activities, legal issues, and religious matters. The noncustodial parent also has other rights, which will be discussed in later sections of this chapter and in chapter 10.

Shared legal custody is an arrangement in which both parents are responsible for making educational, legal, religious, and major medical decisions for the child.

Here are three common custody arrangements:

+ Parents share both legal and physical custody.

+ One parent has primary physical custody, but they share legal custody.

+ One parent has both sole legal custody and primary physical custody.

Sharing custody is predicated on parents' ability to communicate, cooperate, and make joint decisions about their child's welfare. In cases in which co-parents demonstrate that they cannot cooperate and communicate well enough to properly care for their children together, they may be ordered by a judge to attend co-parenting classes. (In some states, co-parenting classes are mandated as part of divorce proceedings for all couples with children.) If the failure to cooperate and communicate persists, the judge may find one or both parents in contempt and may award one parent sole legal and/or physical custody. In some other cases, one parent is given sole legal custody because the parents live so far apart that joint decision making would be impractical.

Common Parenting Time Schedules

Which of the following parenting time schedules appeals to you, and why? Which do you think your ex would prefer? Which do you think your child would prefer? Ultimately, you'll need to weigh all these considerations and choose a schedule that is in your child's best interest.

+ Alternating weeks: Child spends one week with Parent A, followed by one week with Parent B.

+ A 2/2/5/5 schedule: Child spends two days with Parent A, two days with Parent B, five days with Parent A and then five days with Parent B.

+ A 3/3/4/4 schedule: Same as 2/2/5/5, except the rotation is for three and four days.

+ Child lives primarily with Parent A during the school year and primarily with Parent B during the summer and other school breaks.

+ Child spends weekends (or every other weekend) plus one or more evenings with Parent A and the rest of the time with Parent B. This arrangement is common in families in which one parent has primary physical custody, with the nonresidential parent as Parent A; weekends may or may not be part of Parent B's parenting time.

Some parents of infants or young children prefer a schedule that involves less back and forth between houses. As their children get older, they may decide to revisit the schedule to accommodate their children's changing needs.

Teenagers may prefer to go back and forth less often than they did when they were younger. They might prefer an alternating-weeks schedule to a 2/2/5/5 schedule, for example. Also, depending upon how the emotionally turbulent time of adolescence plays out in each household, a teen may choose to live primarily with one parent. Such changes in the parenting time schedule during the teen years may be short- or long-term changes. Parents will need to decide how flexible to be in the face of a teen's request to change the parenting time schedule. Is the request simply motivated by the teen's desire to avoid the stricter parent's house rules? Or would more time in one household actually benefit her emotionally, socially, educationally, or otherwise?

Parents who have more than one child may choose to build provisions into their schedule that allow each parent to have one-on-one time with each child. In our family, we alternate one-on-one weekly dinners with our daughters on Tuesday nights. On occasion, we also have what the girls call "split weekends," where one child is at each house on Friday night and then they switch the next night. Or one child may spend an entire weekend with Mike while the other child is with Deesha.

When co-parents live in different states, the schedule may consist of one of the following or a combination of two or more:

- The child spends one weekend or more each month at the nonresidential parent's home.

- The nonresidential parent comes to the child's primary city of residence one or more weekends a month.

- The child spends all or part of the summer with the nonresidential parent, along with certain holidays and long holiday weekends during the school year

Other parenting time schedule considerations are presented in chapter 8.

Here's our family's basic parenting time schedule:

Mike	Deesha
Sunday night (including on Deesha's weekend)	Tuesday night
Monday night	Wednesday night
Thursday night	Alternating weekends
Alternating weekends	

During their summer break, the girls (when they aren't in camp) are primarily with Deesha during the day (while Mike is at work), because she works from home.

Nesting

"Nesting" is the name given to a co-parenting arrangement in which the children remain in the family home while their parents rotate in and out of the house according to their parenting time schedule. One co-parenting mom who is nesting with her ex-husband blogs anonymously about her family's experiences at www.thiscuckoosnest.com. Her story below, previously published on our *Co-Parenting 101* blog (Philyaw and Thomas 2012), illustrates not only the particulars of a nesting arrangement, but also how detailed planning, cooperation, and communication are essential building blocks of a successful postdivorce parenting partnership.

> My ex-husband and I are attempting Bird's Nest Custody. I say "attempting" because it is an up and down process but we are both committed to making this work for our three young children for as long as we can.
>
> We went to marriage counseling for eight months, and finally admitted to each other that our marriage would

never be happy. We were not going to grow old together. We wanted different things.

On that day in therapy, we were both tearful but had finally reached the point that we could look at each other and ask, "What about the children?" With the therapist looking on, we agreed that we had two options that some couples don't have, primarily because we weren't angry at each other (although admittedly we were disappointed with each other in spades). We could stay together for another ten years to give the children an intact home for as long as we could, or we could split now and try to make it as good for the children as possible.

I am a licensed clinical social worker and have done a significant portion of my professional work in pediatrics at a world-renowned hospital. I have seen every possible custody arrangement and read more custody paperwork than I can count prior to sending it upstairs to the hospital attorney. I have myself had to supervise visitation, at a judge's order, of a dying child because the parents could not get along even when the child was taking his last breaths. I have seen many couples that had to exchange their children at the sheriff's department, with our patient hooked up to an IV pole, because their relationship was so volatile. I did not want that for my children.

On the Internet I found just enough information on Bird's Nest Custody to pique my interest, but admittedly most of it was negative. I spoke about it with a friend who is a family law attorney, who had "sort of heard of it" but not in our area. Our mediator had heard of it several times but had never heard of it used for anything more than a transitional arrangement. My attorney thought it was a "novel" idea but was concerned that it would be a tough sell to a judge. Apparently, judges don't care how your plan works, but they do not want you to end up back on their docket. Custody arrangements with such frequent contact between ex-spouses raise a red flag. My attorney explained their reservations in this way: They view more spousal contact as an increased risk of conflict which increases the chance that you will end up back in their court room. He cautioned me that we would need to get the "right" judge to sign off on our parenting plan.

My ex-husband and I had a few things that we agreed upon fully regarding our children. First, the failure of our marriage was *not their failure, it was our failure* and therefore we should bear the brunt of the inconvenience of our divorce. Second, we wanted to minimize the disruption to their lives. We both agreed that we should stress to the children that we did not have to be married anymore to still be a family. Forever we are their family. We wanted them to see that we would be standing together with the same expectations that we had for them before. When we broke the news of our divorce to the children, we both tearfully stressed to them that we were going to do everything that we could to make this arrangement work and to prove that we were still a close family.

We have now been bird nesting for fourteen months. The fundamental basis of bird nesting is that the children have the home. They sleep every night in their own beds, surrounded by all of their belongings, eat at the family table, do their homework in the same place each night and play with the family dog. My ex-husband and I rotate in and out of the nest as described by our parenting plan. He comes in, and I go out. Both of us do have our separate spaces in the nest. We had an office/small den downstairs that he has taken for his room and I have our old bedroom upstairs. Thus far, we both respect the other's spaces. We have both managed to avoid getting a separate apartment, primarily because we are never off more than two or three nights. I stay in my parents' spare room on my off nights or spread myself among supportive friends.

Our permanent parenting plan works like this:
Mother has Mon. and Tues. evenings

Father has Wed. and Thurs. evenings

Mother has the weekend, Friday, Saturday, and Sunday until 5 p.m.

During the next week…

Father is on Mon. and Tues. evenings

Mother is on Wed. and Thurs. evenings

Father has the weekend, Friday, Saturday and Sunday until 5 p.m.

We have every other weekend with the children and neither of us ever goes longer than two or three nights out of the nest.

Financially, we have both committed to maintain the nest for the children, and we both still own the house. In determining our financial arrangement, we agreed with our mediator that it should be on a pro rata basis. Both of us work full-time, but my ex-husband makes 68 percent of our household income, I make 32 percent. We determined the cost of running the nest, including: mortgage, utilities, cable, groceries, kid expenses (clothes, school supplies, braces, etc.), our life insurance policies, the house cleaning service that comes every two weeks, the kids' college fund contributions, etc. Every month, he deposits 68 percent and I deposit 32 percent of that number. Neither of us can make a withdrawal from that account. If we spend over $200 out of the nest account we have to consult the other party. Any additional expenses that come up that we haven't accounted for [fall] under the 68/32 rule. Both of us have a vested interest in keeping the nest in good order since it remains a joint asset.

There are some nest rules that we both follow.

1. Respect the other's private space in the nest.

2. Leave the nest like you found it. (This is our biggest source of conflict.)

3. No overnight guests of the opposite sex in the nest. They may visit but need to be gone by kid's bedtime. If someone gets remarried, this will have to be revisited.

4. The parent that is on "nest duty" is in charge of the nest. We have an agreement that if the other parent wants to drop by or stay for dinner, it is at the discretion of the parent on. If at any point that parent requests you leave, you leave.

We have found some major perks to nesting. We do spend more time as a family than we would if we weren't rotating so often. Quite often if the parent rotating off is not in a hurry to leave, we all eat together or watch TV with the kids. It has been very helpful to me to have him available for homework; if our sixth-grader has math that I find impossible, his father (who may be just leaving) can sit and help. But by mutual agreement, the parent not on nest duty is not responsible for dinner, homework, or anything in the nest. If you are off, you are off. If you want to stay and the other one doesn't mind, then by all means stay.

Our arrangement has also evolved to the point that we have some "deals" not in the legal paperwork. For example, the parent that is on for the weekend goes at some point during the weekend and buys groceries for the nest for the week. Our children take their lunch to school and so this guarantees that someone doesn't wake up to make lunches and find nothing there. In addition, at times I find myself doing his laundry but he is responsible for the yard. As I have folded his shirts, at times with some resentment, I have [had] to remind myself that I didn't rake one leaf during the fall.

Our agreement also contains provisions for "nesting gone bad." If one parent wants out of the nesting agreement, for remarriage or any other circumstance, then we can re-evaluate at any point and either sell or buy the other parent out of the house. Both of us have verbalized our intent to make this work for as long as possible. Considering that our youngest child is seven we have a long way to go.

We recognize that nesting would never work for many divorcing couples. You have to be able to get along and you have to be able to put a lot of old emotional baggage from your relationship down for your children. This would never work for high-conflict couples.

Nesting is not always convenient for us as parents. We both are in other romantic relationships, and these new partners also have to understand our responsibility to the nest. Yes, I have a bag that is always half packed in my closet. But I feel better knowing that as an adult, I can manage the burden of the bag better than my children.

Right of First Refusal

What if there are times when you can't care for your children during your parenting time due to work obligations or other schedule conflicts? In the interest of maximizing the children's time with both parents, consider asking your co-parent to care for the kids before seeking child care elsewhere. Family courts call this process "first option" or "right of first refusal," and when co-parents agree to it—or a judge orders it—provisions for exercising this option are included in the parenting plan. If there's a significant other, roommate, or older sibling who can routinely care for your children in your absence, you may choose not to include this clause in your agreement; it may simply be more convenient for a child to stay where he is normally scheduled to be. However, if the available parent has limited parenting time to begin with or if your schedule conflict is ongoing, first refusal may be in your child's best interest.

If you and your co-parent are willing to not only cover for each other, but actually swap days (or nights), your child won't miss any time with either of you. When you give your ex first refusal or swap to make up lost time, not only are you doing your ex a favor, you're doing your child a favor as well.

Flexibility

First option is one example of the kind of flexibility that benefits children in co-parenting families. While keeping to a routine is best for parents and children, some flexibility in your parenting time schedule allows your children's needs to be met as your children get older and as they adjust to living across two households. Over the years since we first separated, our basic parenting time schedule has been tweaked on several occasions to accommodate changes in our children's lives. We also temporarily alter the schedule at times when one or both of our children need more time with one of us. For example, a few months before Mike's wedding, both girls expressed a desire to spend an extra weeknight with him. Of course, neither of us is ever thrilled to lose time with our kids, but we see how they thrive with the new arrangement; we accept that divorce and co-parenting means everyone in our family makes compromises and sacrifices at various times, and, as parents, we gladly aim to take the lion's share of those compromises and sacrifices.

Also, now that we are co-parenting a teenager, we allow her to have more of a choice about which parent she's with and when. With some ground rules, such as discussing any potential changes with both parents first, we're able to honor her wishes and still maintain order in our daily lives.

In some families, the parenting time schedule changes permanently or temporarily in response to changes in school, career, or health circumstances for parents and for kids, or to support the kids' participation in extracurricular activities or special events. Schedule changes and swaps require communication and compromise, so co-parents who experience a high level of conflict may have a formal or informal agreement not to make any changes to the parenting time schedule. Unfortunately, this means their children may miss out on special events or opportunities. So think of flexibility as a gift you can give your children that will make living in two households feel like less of a punishment.

And remember to reward your ex's flexibility with courtesy. If you need to swap or need him to cover for you, ask in a timely fashion, with the understanding that he is not obligated to accommodate your request.

Pick-Up and Drop-Off Times and Locations

Several factors come into play when deciding the where, when, and who of picking up and dropping off your children for transitions between houses. Which parent should drop off or pick up? Is one house more convenient than the other for drop-off or pick-up? Or is a midway point or other location a better choice? Is it harder for your child to see one parent leave than the other? The answers to these questions may change as time passes and as your child grows older and adjusts to the transitions—and as you as co-parents grow and transition as well.

Before we became neighbors (as mentioned in chapter 1), Mike lived around the corner from Deesha. Despite the short distance, he would pick up the girls from Deesha's house because it was on his way home from work. For a while, it wasn't easy for him to enter the house in which we had once lived together. But he pushed past his discomfort and went inside each time, to make things as comfortable as possible for the girls. Deesha welcomed him inside, for the same reason. Eventually, the awkwardness faded, and we both began to take transitions in stride. Our children did too.

Now that we are neighbors, our children simply walk down the street and transition themselves from house to house at the scheduled times.

In high-conflict situations, some co-parents choose (or are ordered by the court) to drop off and pick up in public locations or to have a relative or friend take the child. One co-parent in our Facebook group meets her ex in store parking lots because they have security cameras. In extremely volatile cases, co-parents may be required to conduct transitions at a police station.

Other locations—libraries, gas stations, grocery stores—may also be preferable simply for the sake of convenience.

Generally speaking, drop-off and pick-up times should be coordinated in a way that respects each parent's scheduled parenting time and gives the children enough time to get settled into the home at which they are arriving, reconnect with that parent, and get proper rest for the next day.

Transitions

Even co-parents who are civil at other times may find the face-to-face nature of transitions a challenge. You may find it awkward, uncomfortable, sad, or enraging to be in the presence of your ex. You may be upset about being without your children for several days. Maybe your ex is seriously behind in child support. But transitions are not the time for confrontations or otherwise wearing your feelings on your sleeve. Your children are counting on you to conduct yourself peacefully and to help them through what is likely an emotionally challenging time for them too. Your tears, angry face, angry words, eye rolls, or stony silence can saddle your child with fears and doubts, such as:

+ *I'm making Daddy mad because I'm leaving.*

+ *I can't let Mommy see that I'm excited to be going to Daddy's house.*

+ *Mommy is going to miss me too much. I shouldn't leave her. But if I don't go, Dad will be upset...*

Your child shouldn't have to bear the burden of such thoughts. Remember, co-parents do the brunt of the heavy emotional lifting so that the children won't have to do as much. Use the tips presented in previous chapters to help you work through any difficult emotions you experience at transitions. And in the meantime, do as one member of our Facebook group advised: "Fake it until you make it." If your time with your child is at an end, give your child permission to go with your co-parent and have a good time, even though you'll miss each other. Put on your game face, cry in the car after your child has left, do whatever you need to do to hold it together so that your child is truly free—emotionally free—to go with the other parent and enjoy herself.

What if it's your *child*, and not you, who is reluctant to part at times of transition? First, listen to what your child has to say about her reluctance to leave, if she's able and willing to articulate her feelings. Empathize with her and affirm her feelings of sadness or frustration, her wish that things were like they used to be before the divorce, or other concerns. Remember that feelings aren't right or wrong, so try to offer encouragement and comfort without trying to change how she feels about the transitions. By listening, you can determine whether the issue is something that you, the other parent, or both of you working together can address.

For a younger child who cannot articulate his concerns and who continually exhibits behavioral problems before, during, or after transitions, we recommend consulting with your pediatrician or family counselor.

Children of all ages may have difficulty articulating that the reason they don't want to transition is because one or both parents' verbal and nonverbal messages are making it difficult for them to do so. Your words and actions during your parenting time as well as during transitions can influence—for better or for worse—your child's feelings about spending time with the other parent. If your child senses (or sees outright) that you are angry or upset about it, she may become ambivalent, resistant, or fearful about leaving you.

When a child says, "But I don't want to go!" it may be tempting for a well-meaning, concerned parent to make the parenting plan or court order the "fall guy" by telling the child she has to go because the court says so. Unfortunately, this explanation, however true, may make the child feel even less secure and in control of her life than she already does. Not only have her parents broken up and forever changed her family life, but now some "court" is controlling all of them. Blaming the court may leave your child feeling hopeless and vulnerable. Instead, offer her the reassurance that you will do what you can to address the underlying issues so that spending time with both parents will be something that she looks forward to.

Holidays and School Breaks

Holidays, unfortunately, don't fit neatly into a parenting time schedule, so special provisions must be made. In advance, you and your co-parent will need to decide where your child will spend summer vacation, school breaks, and major and minor holidays.

In our family, the girls are with Mike for Thanksgiving in odd-numbered years and for New Year's Eve in even-numbered years. We all spend Christmas Eve and Christmas Day together. Our daughters enjoy two weeks off from school during the winter and two weeks off for spring break. They spend one week per break with each of us. During the summer we adhere to the regular schedule except for two weeks when we each have one full week with the girls.

The girls spend Mother's Day with Deesha and Father's Day with Mike, even if this requires deviating from the regular schedule. The remaining holidays are divided in a variety of ways. For holidays such as Memorial Day and Martin Luther King Jr. Day, we try to alternate throughout the year in sequential order, so that we each get roughly the same number of long weekends with our kids. Sometimes this requires tweaking the parenting time schedule to get our alternating weekends back on track.

Birthdays

You and your co-parent may choose to host a birthday party together for your child each year and take turns organizing it; have one parent host a party on odd-numbered years, and the other on even-numbered years; or celebrate your child's birthday during your regularly scheduled parenting time. The logic behind not hosting two parties in a given year is that, presumably, the same guests would be invited to both parties, which would be confusing to invitees and could result in one party being poorly attended.

Some parenting plans also make provisions for the children to spend time with parents on the parents' birthdays.

We try to refrain from being heavy-handed in our advice to co-parents, but...*never, ever, ever crash a birthday party thrown for your child by the other parent.* If you're not invited, don't show up. If you're invited but your new significant other is not, don't bring that person with you. However much you loathe your ex for not inviting you, love your child enough not to risk making a scene on his special day. Because even if you show up and act civilly, you can't guarantee that your ex's response to your unwelcome presence will be civil. Instead, host your own party or celebrate your child's birthday in another way. The day of the birthday party is only one day; you will have many more days to show your child that she is special and important to you. Some co-parents choose to celebrate half-birthdays to avoid such conflicts.

Sadly, we've heard from several co-parents that they've been forbidden to attend their child's birthday party and then later asked by their child why they didn't attend. If you feel compelled to bar the other parent from your child's party, be honest with your child about your decision. If you can't take responsibility for the fallout from your decision, then perhaps you should reconsider.

Clothing and Other Items

One of the decisions we made at the outset of our separation is that our children would not have to carry suitcases back and forth between houses. We wanted them to always feel as if both houses are "home," complete with everything they need, and that they aren't merely visiting one or the other. They sometimes take specific clothing items, toys, or books with them to the other house, but otherwise, they have all the clothes and toiletries they need at both houses. This means that when Deesha takes the kids clothes shopping, half the clothes immediately go to Mike's house. In the beginning, each of us took responsibility for washing the kids' clothes at our respective houses. Now that the kids are older, they are primarily responsible for their own laundry.

Who will be responsible for buying and laundering your kids' clothes? Will your child's wardrobe be split between houses, or will he need to bring a suitcase when transitioning? Will your child be expected to bring certain clothes items back after being at the other (or your) house? If so, who is responsible for making sure those items come back—your child or the other parent?

Clothing can become a point of contention for co-parents. Keeping up with your child's clothes requires diligence, and inevitably children forget and lose things. On the flip side, if your child does transport her clothing back and forth, it's important that you make a good-faith effort to see that she returns to the other house with everything she needs.

If you are flexible and allow your child to take a few special toys and books between houses, it can make transitions easier. But it also creates the need for someone to be responsible for making sure the beloved items stay with the child. As your child grows older, he can take on more and more of this responsibility himself.

In addition to clothes and special items the kids may wish to take between houses, you may want to exchange school papers, kids' artwork, mail, and other documents during transitions. During the years that Mike picked the girls up from Deesha's house, Deesha kept a basket in the foyer that the kids dubbed the "Dad Basket." Deesha and the girls put items they wanted Mike to see or sign into the basket. This prevented us from having to rush around at pick-up time trying to find things.

Money Matters

If either parent owes the other child support, the amount will be determined by state guidelines or negotiated. Your parenting plan may articulate the specifics of any child support orders.

There are also expenses not covered by child support, such as work-related child care and medical and dental insurance, to consider. Who will be responsible for these? Also, who will pay for camps, other extracurricular activities, or other expenses that may arise? If you and your co-parent will divide these expenses, will it be 50-50 or a different split?

You'll also need to decide which of you will claim the children when filing your tax return. Some parents alternate years; in the case of two children, some parents each claim one of the children every year.

Education and Extracurricular Activities

When parents share legal custody, they share responsibility for making decisions related to the child's education. If only one parent has legal custody, that parent is responsible for this decision making, including deciding where the child will attend school. However, courts generally maintain that the choice of school cannot place an unfair financial burden on the noncustodial parent. Also, the noncustodial parent has a right to receive information in a timely fashion from the custodial parent about the child's grades and school activities. The noncustodial parent is also entitled to receive copies of school records, to participate in parent-teacher conferences, and to attend graduation ceremonies. The noncustodial parent should also be listed as a parent and as an emergency contact on registration and other forms. During her parenting time, a noncustodial parent may take the child to school, pick him up from school, or take him to other activities, unless a court order or the parenting plan says otherwise.

It's best for the kids if the responsibility for homework does not fall to only one parent if the children regularly spend time in both homes. For younger children, this requires parents to communicate with each other and to help the children stay organized and on top of due dates, obtain materials needed for projects, and have time to study.

Camps and other extracurricular activities should be chosen with the child's best interest in mind. Therefore, they should not be scheduled to intentionally disrupt one parent's parenting time. However, both parents should support their child's involvement in enrichment opportunities by being willing to take her to games, lessons, and other events during their parenting time.

Just as parenting time is not contingent upon payment of child support, child support is not an admission price a parent must pay in order to attend a child's activities. Unless a judge rules otherwise, noncustodial parents have the right to attend their children's school functions and special events. And children have the right to enjoy these occasions without disruptive behavior from either parent. It is hurtful and disrespectful for one parent to discourage the other from supporting a child in this way.

"My ex-husband has this fiction in his head that says because I left him and no longer care for him, I don't care about our sons," said one co-parenting mom. "And he actually tells them this nonsense. Then I have to find out from other sources—or from the boys— about their soccer games and other activities. He won't tell me because he doesn't want me there. And when I do show up, he wants to make a scene. So I'm torn between being there for my kids—and risking him acting like a jackass and upsetting the boys—and not being there. If I'm not there, he tells the kids, 'See, I told you that your mama doesn't care about you.' So I'm damned if I do, damned if I don't."

Your child's soccer game is not the place to squabble over co-parenting logistics or to air complaints. Focus on your child, not each other. Games, school functions, and other activities are the rare occasions on which your child can have both parents in the same place; allow him to have this special time without drama. Being civil toward your ex—even if she acts otherwise—will help make these occasions memorable for your child, for all the right reasons.

Health and Medical Issues

Parents with shared legal custody make joint decisions regarding their children's health. If only one parent has legal custody, that parent is responsible for making health decisions. However, the noncustodial parent has a right to receive information in a timely fashion from the custodial parent about the children's health and well-being and is entitled to copies of the children's medical records. Also, the noncustodial parent should be listed as a parent and as an emergency contact on health-related forms.

If your child has special needs that require medical or educational services, determine how you and your co-parent will handle the time and cost associated with these services.

Travel

Here are just a few of the travel-related considerations that should be addressed in your parenting plan:

+ How will the child travel to spend time with the nonresidential parent—by car or airplane? If by airplane, will parents share the cost of the round-trip ticket and will the child be escorted during the flight? Who will pay for the escort's ticket?

+ Will the parents share the travel costs for all trips, or just for the summer break?

While a noncustodial parent may take a child to visit with friends and family or go on vacation, only a parent with legal custody may apply for a passport for the child. However, once a passport has been obtained, one parent cannot prevent the other parent from taking the child out of the country unless there is a court order barring that parent from international travel with the child. Airports may require proof of permission to travel overseas when a child is traveling with only one parent. See the US Customs and Border Protection website (help.cbp.gov/app/home) for more information.

Special Considerations for Teens

Co-parenting teenagers brings unique questions and challenges, such as:

+ Are you willing to have a more flexible or informal parenting time schedule?

+ At what age will your child be allowed to date? To drive? To get a job?

+ Will your child have her own car? Who will be responsible for maintenance and insurance for the car?

+ Who is responsible for paying for college?

Other Considerations

Here are some additional questions that you and your co-parent should proactively address:

+ Who will stay home with the kids when they are sick?

+ Who will take the kids to routine doctor and dentist appointments?

+ How will military service (if applicable) impact your co-parenting arrangement?

+ What happens if you or your co-parent relocates outside of your current school district?

+ What happens if one of you relocates out of state?

+ What are the conditions under which children will be introduced to a parent's new significant other? (See chapter 11 for
  a detailed discussion of co-parenting and dating.)

+ Do you have stipulations about overnight guests when children are present?

Calendars and Other Organizational Tools

Managing the details of your parenting partnership can feel overwhelming. Because our own co-parenting arrangement is rather
simple and informal, a shared online calendar (available free at www.
google.com/calendar) is sufficient to help us stay organized. Our
respective parenting times are marked on the calendar along with the
girls' appointments, school events, and extracurricular activities. For
convenience, Google Calendar allows users to create multiple, over-
lapping calendars that appear on a single screen. So we can input our
personal and professional schedules along with the parenting time
schedule, with the assurance that the other parent will see only the
kid-related entries because that's the only calendar that we share. We
can both make changes to the shared calendar.

Some parents choose to use, or are required by the courts to use,
an online custody organizer to keep track of the parenting time
schedule and other important information related to their parenting
plan. Such organizers can be easily found through an online search.
Some are free of charge, while others offer a limited amount of service
for free with additional features available for a fee. Some organizers
allow you to track expenses, post correspondence for the other parent,
and maintain an online co-parenting journal.

Once you and your co-parent have finalized the details as to how you will parent across two households, your intentions should be formalized into a parenting plan. Some family courts require co-parents to create such a plan as part of their custody proceedings. In the next chapter, we'll take a look at some of the questions and considerations that will inform your parenting plan.

Chapter 8

Write Your Own Parenting Plan

Parents know the most about the child and the child's
needs. Parents are also aware of their parenting strengths.
The parenting plan should be based on both parents'
strengths in meeting the child's needs.

—from the Missouri Bar Parenting Plan Guidelines

Whether your parenting plan is court-mandated or you voluntarily
wish to formalize, and hopefully simplify, the logistics of your co-
parenting arrangement, you can start by drafting a proposal.
Preparing a draft can help you clarify what's important to you and
identify potential sticking points between you and your co-parent. It
can also help you save money, because completing this preliminary
step means your lawyer (if you have or plan on getting one) won't have
to do it.

Consideration of the following factors is vital to a child-centered parenting plan:

+ Each child's temperament, age, developmental stage, daily schedule, and adjustment to the breakup and the subsequent social changes (for example, a new school or new neighborhood)

+ Any special educational, medical, or emotional needs that a child may have

+ Each parent's caregiving role prior to the breakup

As you work out the logistics of shared parenting and care for your child, remember that what may be most comfortable or convenient for you may not necessarily be in your child's best interest. For example, you may miss your child when he is with the other parent and prefer that he spend most of his time with you. Or, you may not want to drive the distance to pick up or drop off at the other parent's house. But your child needs significant time with both fit and willing parents, so compromises and sacrifices must be made. And while parents aren't obligated to deny their needs and feelings in deference to their children's, there will be times when you're called upon to be uncomfortable or shoulder a burden so that your children don't have to.

As there is a lot of information to be organized in the plan, you may wish to consult a sample plan such as the one offered by the Family Court Services of the Third Judicial District of Idaho. This site (familycourtservicesidaho.org) also includes specific information for:

+ Co-parenting schedules for holidays and other special occasions

+ Parenting plan guidelines for children at different ages

+ Parenting plan guidelines for parents who live 30 or more miles apart

+ Supervised visits (when there is a court order for a third party to be present while the child is with the parent)

If it's feasible, you may suggest that your co-parent work with you on drafting the plan, or she may opt to draft her own.

Guiding Questions

In addition to keeping the above considerations in mind, you may find it helpful to review the topics covered in chapter 7 and to answer the guiding questions below when preparing your draft.

1. As co-parents, what commitments do you wish to make to your child? While a parenting plan covers many logistics of co-parenting, such as pick-up and drop-off times, many plans also include more holistic statements about parental responsibility and children's rights. Such statements affirm the child's right to and need for basic care, love, and affection from both parents and the freedom to communicate with both parents. These statements also articulate parents' mutual responsibility to:

   + Provide for the child's basic needs.

   + Communicate and cooperate with each other, sharing any important information regarding the child's well-being.

   + Keep the child out of the middle of their conflicts.

   + Protect the child from their adult concerns and disappointments.

   + Avoid using the child as a messenger or interrogating the child about the other parent.

   + Encourage the child's relationship with the other parent.

- Avoid hindering the child's relationship with the other parent.

- Avoid words and actions that would erode the love and respect the child has for the other parent.

2. How will you share parenting responsibilities?

3. What is each parent's availability and capacity to serve as a caregiver? Are both parents able to provide basic care according to the child's age and needs, including school attendance and homework, and attention to any special needs?

4. How does each parent's work schedule influence the parenting time schedule?

5. Does the distance between the child's school and each parent's home and workplace influence the parenting time schedule?

6. Who will be responsible for drop-offs and pick-ups? At what times? Will the times differ for holiday and vacation schedules?

7. If you have more than one child, will they follow the same parenting time schedule, or would they benefit from some time apart?

8. Who will coordinate extracurricular activities?

9. Who will be responsible for child care—either staying at home or arranging other child care—when the child is sick and unable to go to school?

10. Who will schedule and take the child to medical and dental appointments?

11. Who pays for extraordinary expenses, such as braces?

12. What is the deadline for parents to choose their vacation dates with the child?

13. Will both parents celebrate the child's birthday together with a single party, or will you alternate years and take turns hosting a party?

14. Are one or both parents active-duty military? If so, what will be the caregiving arrangements if one or both parents are deployed or are on leave?

15. Can you agree not to use the presence of a new partner as grounds to interfere with the other parent's parenting time?

16. What steps will you take to engage or reengage a co-parent who has previously been uninvolved in or absent from your child's life but who seeks to be involved?

17. What steps toward resolution will you take in case you and your ex don't agree on a particular issue?

18. What are your child's preferences with regard to the parenting time schedule?

19. What sacrifices will you need to make in order to adhere to the parenting time schedule and agreement?

20. How and when will you discuss the details of your parenting plan with your child?

21. How might the parenting time schedule or other arrangements for your child change in the future?

Proactively addressing common and frustrating co-parenting challenges can minimize the need to constantly negotiate. This approach can also lay the groundwork for parents' and children's rights to be honored and for children's needs to be met. While a highly detailed plan can certainly benefit even congenial co-parents, it is ideal for co-parents who find themselves disagreeing more than they agree or for situations where there is hostility and resistance to sharing custody. A detailed plan also allows you to stipulate arrangements for the children at different ages, recognizing that as they get older, certain aspects of your co-parenting situation may need to change.

Once you've completed your draft, review it with your attorney (if you have one). Then, go over it with your co-parent, if possible. You may wish to enlist the services of a mediator, if this isn't already mandated by the court. Highlight the areas of the plan that are priorities for you, and be prepared to negotiate. Remember that if you and your co-parent cannot come to a final decision on certain core issues, a family court judge will do it for you. Be sure to negotiate in good faith so that you as parents remain in control of decisions affecting your family.

Once finalized, your draft will become a parenting plan to be signed by both parents and filed with the court.

Communicating beyond the Plan

Having a plan in place limits the need for co-parents to constantly negotiate and, therefore—hopefully—limits occasion for conflict to arise. Where the kids are supposed to be, when, and for how long... it's all spelled out in the plan. However, it is still in the children's best interest that there be some communication between co-parents. Schedules change, plans change, jobs change, children grow and their needs change, and unpredictable circumstances arise. Some change to the plan—formal or informal—is inevitable.

In your professional life, there are some tasks you just can't outsource. Communication in co-parenting is like that: you're the only man or woman for the job. Your child should not be used as a messenger, and your new spouse or significant other is not an appropriate proxy either. While Deesha can attest to the fact that it's sometimes more convenient and efficient to communicate with Mike's wife, Sherry, she still communicates primarily with Mike about the children. Some co-parents, however, attempt to force the other parent to communicate primarily or exclusively with (or through) their new spouse or partner. Forcing communication between a parent and a stepparent is not in a child's best interest, but some co-parents resort to this because the level of conflict between the co-parents is so high. Unfortunately, this arrangement often serves to fan, not extinguish, the flames of hostility. Other co-parents insist on this arrangement simply because they know it will upset the other parent. Yet others do it to allow the stepparent to assert control or to feel more secure and empowered in the blended family. Regardless of the motivation behind the arrangement, children's needs are not served by it.

If you're in a high-conflict co-parenting situation, communicating with your ex may be the last thing you want to do. This is when being a Business Partner (see chapter 4) can come in handy. Approach the situation the way you would if you had to communicate with a challenging colleague or client about, say, changing the date of an important meeting. You would recognize that avoidance comes with negative consequences, and you'd bite the bullet and do your job, professionally, maturely, and respectfully.

What If My Ex Doesn't Follow the Plan?

If your ex doesn't adhere to the plan you've agreed to, *you* still have an obligation to do so. In chapter 12, we offer some strategies for addressing violations of the parenting plan.

Chapter 9

Separate but Equal

Going to Daddy's house is like spring and summer. Going to Mommy's house is like fall and winter. I like all of [the seasons].

—our daughter Peyton, age 8

Unless you were cloned, you and your co-parent have different personalities, different interests, and possibly different parenting styles. In fact, your differences may have contributed to your breakup. So how do you form a working partnership with someone who's so different from you, across two different households? How do you reconcile your co-parent's TV addiction, and your fears that the kids are following suit, with your Luddite lifestyle? Or her love of fast food with your veganism? What if you're cool with the kids just drifting off to sleep when they get tired, but your co-parent insists on an eight o'clock bedtime?

Getting on the same page as much as possible is worth a conversation with your co-parent. Similar routines and expectations at both houses will make transitions go more smoothly for your children and for both of you. As a bonus, you'll also be affirming each other's parenting choices in your child's eyes by communicating values and expectations that complement, instead of contradict, each other. If something is acceptable at one house but not the other, your child may be uncertain as to what behavior is acceptable in other settings. If she can jump on the couch at Mom's but not at Dad's, will she jump on the couch at a friend's house?

Similar, not identical, experiences are the goal. "My ex and I do try for some consistency," said Jessica, a mom of two boys, "but it's [also] important for children to realize that there are going to be different rules and ways of doing things at Mom's house than at Dad's, just because we're different people and value different things."

You and your co-parent may disagree about the kind of clothing your child is allowed to wear, whether she can get her ears or other body parts pierced, and the age at which she is allowed to date. Some co-parents give in to the temptation of being the hero, seeing themselves as rescuing their children from the "uptight" parent, or being the "fun parent" who is the overindulgent yin to the other parent's more limit-setting yang. Not only is this confusing for a child, but it can make the other parent's job tougher than it has to be.

"My ex-husband is a classic Disney Dad," said Amanda, a mom of an eighth-grade boy. "Trips, eating out every night, video games all day…if my son asks for it, his dad buys it for him. So [my son] appreciates nothing. Meanwhile, no homework is getting done. So when [my son] comes back to my house and his grades are in the toilet, I have to be the bad guy, the disciplinarian. I'm the one getting the e-mails from his teachers. I'm the only parent telling him 'No' and expecting anything of him. He gets one message from me and another from his dad, and my message of responsibility and doing well in school is not sticking. And when I told him the other day to clean his filthy room, he had the nerve to ask me why I don't just get housecleaning service like his dad has!"

Amanda may make more headway with her ex if she starts by discussing their son's abysmal grades than if she launches into what her ex may perceive as an attack on him as a parent. By framing the topic as a way to facilitate the transitions between households for your child and to help him become more successful academically and in the long term, you may find your co-parent more receptive than if you appear to be criticizing her lifestyle and parenting choices.

While children do well when their environments are consistent, the two households that your children are a part of need not be identical. Children are also quite adaptable to new ways of doing things. The differences between houses require co-parents to adapt to a new reality as well: you cannot control what happens in the other parent's house and during the other parent's parenting time.

His House, His Rules

One of the most essential—and for some co-parents, the most frustrating—truths about co-parenting is this: You have to relinquish control of some of the details of your child's life. In the eyes of the family court system, co-parents generally have no say as to what happens in the other parent's home unless there is some harm being done to the children. Therefore, you can't control your ex's interactions with your child. You can't control what meals are served or what TV shows your child watches at your ex's house. You also can't control whom your ex dates or your ex's new significant other's interactions with your child.

Make a list of the differences you're aware of between your household and parenting style and your ex's. Consider each item on the list, and ask yourself whether your child's *basic* needs are being met in both homes. Using this criterion can reduce the "my way versus your way" bickering that co-parents can easily fall into. Take note of any serious issues that need to be discussed with your ex.

Of course, reasonable parents may disagree about what constitutes "serious" or harm. So how do you know which concerns to raise with your co-parent and which to chalk up to "his house, his rules"?

Some co-parents accept (sometimes grudgingly) "his house, his rules" and refrain from discussing *any* concerns. Instead, they focus on what happens during their own parenting time. Rhonda, who was co-parenting her preschool-aged son with her boyfriend, said, "I used to have a panic attack every time my son went with his dad. And I'd say a prayer. There's so much going on over at that house that I just don't agree with. But I got tired of arguing and fighting—and it wasn't getting us anywhere. The same stuff kept happening. So I just decided to work on being the best parent I can be when he's with me. With me, he goes to bed at a decent time, and he doesn't sit in front of the TV all day. I can't control what happens over there, but I can control my own house, and my reactions. So now when his dad does something or neglects to do something, I look at it like this: If I saw my neighbor parenting this same way, would I call Child Protective Services on her? If I wouldn't make that call on my neighbor for that behavior, then I don't say anything to his dad about it. But I still say a prayer when he goes."

"There's a lot happening at my ex-wife's house that concerns me," said Nelson, a dad of two. "She thinks I'm jealous of her new boyfriend, but I'm not. He's just not the type of person I want around my kids. But I wouldn't want her interfering in *my* life, so I don't interfere in hers. My kids seem to be safe and happy, so for now I keep my mouth shut and just focus on them. Their mother's boyfriend is not a role model I'd choose for them, and I could bad-mouth this guy. But instead, through my own character and behavior, I try to show my kids what is appropriate."

Some co-parents tell us that they don't mind hearing concerns from the other parent, as long as they're approached in a respectful manner. "My ex-wife likes to make all sorts of *demands* about what I feed our sons, what time they go to bed…everything," said Jeff, a co-parenting dad of three. "She sees herself as the *real* parent, which really irks me, but I don't mind listening to what she has to say because I know her heart is in the right place. Still, I had to let her know: 'You're not going to make demands on me. We can have a *conversation*, and some things I might do your way, and some things I won't. But as long as you come to me respectfully, I'll always listen.'"

Believe Half of What You Hear

So what do you do when it's your *child* who has a problem with the differences between houses? Lyssa, a co-parenting mom of two, said, "My daughter was quick to tell me, 'But Dad lets me do it.' And I used to tell her, 'I don't care what your dad lets you do. This is my house.' But then I realized that she was genuinely confused about the different rules. So I explained to her that my rules were based on what I think is important and best for her, and that sometimes her dad and I disagree about that. I told her that two people can love the same person, like her dad and I love her, and still not agree about everything. And I had to remember that myself. Now that she's a teenager, we've gotten it down pat: The foul music her dad allows her to listen to doesn't cross the threshold of my front door. I don't even have to say anything; she knows to leave that at his house."

Kids are smart. They quickly figure out that when their parents are on opposite sides of an issue, there may be a way to work the situation to their advantage. "When my daughter came back from her dad's and told me that she hadn't eaten breakfast the entire time she was with him, I was livid," said Cherita, whose daughter was seven at the time. "I remembered how when we were together, he would let her eat junk food for every meal, if he fed her at all, if I didn't intervene. So when she told me this, I immediately picked up the phone and let him have it. Well, it turns out, he had offered her breakfast but she didn't like the cereal he bought. She told him that I didn't allow her to eat cereal for breakfast…which is not true!" There are two lessons to be learned from this: some previously lax parents do rise to the occasion and become more engaged and responsible parents after a breakup, and it's really important that co-parents communicate with each other directly.

Deesha used to teach elementary school. She learned that teachers sometimes tell parents, somewhat tongue in cheek: "If *you* don't believe everything your child tells you about what happened at school, *I* won't believe everything your child tells me about what happens at home." This certainly applies to co-parenting. It's not that you should be inclined to disbelieve what your children tell you about the other parent. Rather, you should also get the other parent's perspective.

It's Not a Competition if You're on the Same Team

"I get so tired of hearing 'Mommy bought me this' and 'Mommy took me to this fancy place' ...I want to say, 'Well, of course Mommy did all that; she takes half of my paycheck every month!" said Nick, a co-parenting dad of an eight-year-old girl. "I can't compete with all of that. I just can't afford it, and I probably still wouldn't do it even if I could."

Nick is wise not to enter into a spending competition with his ex. Despite your best efforts and your co-parent's, it can feel like a competition: your child pitting the experiences she has at one house against the other. But it's okay for children to notice differences; it's your job to teach them that those differences are acceptable. "I tell my son that I'm happy he has a room just for toys in his dad's new house," said Debbie of her son, Alex, and her soon-to-be-ex. "Alex doesn't have a room like that at my house, but that's okay because I don't see it as a competition. His dad and I are on the same team...Alex's."

Whether you're concerned about your child's red meat and dairy intake at Dad's house, or your child is bummed because you don't have the latest gaming system like Mom does, try to take it in stride. When you feel discouraged by all the ways you and your ex differ, and all the things you don't have in common, remember that the one thing the two of you will always have in common is the most important of all: your child. This positive perspective will come in handy when you're faced with co-parenting challenges. In the next chapter, we'll discuss some of the unique challenges that never-married and non-custodial parents face.

Chapter 10

"What about Us?": Never-Married and Noncustodial Parents

Several years ago, I started to look for resources to help me understand how to co-parent in a way that would be healthy for all of us. But most of the books addressed co-parenting after divorce. We were never married. I couldn't really find anything that addressed…parents in our situation. So, I decided to build what I needed, and as I talked to other people about the idea, including my son's father, I found that I wasn't alone.

—Talibah Mbonisi, founder of WeParent (www.weparent.com)

Whether their parents are married or divorced, unmarried or separated, children benefit when both of their parents are actively involved in their lives. While much of the information in the previous chapters is applicable to co-parents regardless of marital status and custody arrangement, there are some issues that co-parents who never married each other and noncustodial parents face that can complicate their co-parenting experience. (Note: We're using "never-married" as a shorthand here, understanding that these co-parents may be, or may have been, married to other people.)

"Baby Mamas" and "Baby Daddies"

"It's awesome having your parenting role reduced to the butt of jokes," says Tori, a never-married mom of three. "And by awesome, I mean terrible. The day I saw 'baby mama' and 'baby daddy' make their way into the pop culture mainstream—on CNN no less—all I could do was shake my head. I mean, I get it: I'm not the wife or even the ex-wife. So I guess I don't deserve 'the mother of his child,' or 'his child's mother,' or even 'Haley's mom.' It's just one more way our society continues to delegitimize—and I hate the whole concept of illegitimacy too—our families and relationships, just because we're not married."

In the United States, 40 percent of children are born to unmarried parents, according to NPR (National Public Radio) (Aslanian 2012). Some of these parents, like Tori, chafe against what they perceive as a lack of respect for their co-parenting roles, embodied in the idioms "baby mama" and "baby daddy." Others, like WeParent founder Talibah Mbonisi, jokingly refer to themselves in this way, but still take issue with the presumptions sometimes thrown around about families like theirs, particularly if they are African-American.

"When the [female] colleague of a friend of mine learned that he is the father of three, she very politely asked him if they all had the same mother!" Mbonisi says. "Yes, she was accusing him of being a baby daddy, and even though she didn't use those words, her question was incredibly loaded" (personal communication, June 2009).

In addition to social stigmas, never-married co-parents may face other challenges:

+ The legitimation process (In many states, a never-married father has no parental rights until a DNA test establishes his paternity; only then may he file for custody and parenting time.)

+ Not having the benefit of a legal or "official" requirement to take co-parenting classes, to work with a mediator, or to have a parenting plan on file until and unless one or both parents choose to engage the family court system

+ Feeling awkward or resentful about co-parenting with someone with whom they had not previously established a commitment or familiarity (Conversely, this could *facilitate* co-parenting, as there's no old relationship baggage to overcome.)

+ Helping their children respond to stigmatization by peers, adults, or institutions because their parents never married

Noting how magazines and TV news stories cheer on single moms such as actresses Sandra Bullock and Halle Berry, never-married co-parenting mom Bridget wonders, "Why do I have to be a celebrity to get some respect as a single mom? As a non-celebrity, I deal with the sideways looks from people when they find out that I'm a single mom. The message single moms get, even from our families sometimes, is that we should be ashamed and that our children are a mistake. I deal with assumptions that my child's father is nowhere to be found. But the truth is, a lot of us are doing a damn good job parenting together, without a marriage license or a divorce decree."

Tori says, "I want what every parent wants. I want my child to feel proud of her family and who she is. And for children to feel that pride and that positive sense of self, it's up to parents to instill it by not feeling ashamed themselves."

Like all co-parents, never-married co-parents are called upon to work through their own fears, discomfort, and frustration with each other in order to parent their children together and help them thrive in a culture that doesn't always validate them.

Noncustodial parents also face a lack of validation in our culture. Below is an interview with Rebekah Spicuglia, a noncustodial parent who is devoted to changing the way noncustodial parents are regarded and empowering them to be an involved presence in their children's lives.

An Interview with Rebekah Spicuglia, Founder of *NonCustodial Parent Community*

The first time we visited the blog NonCustodial Parent Community (NCP Community) (ncp-community.blogspot.com), *the first thing that caught our eye was a picture of* NCP Community *founder Rebekah Spicuglia and her son, smiling—actually, beaming—for the camera. The caption read, "This is what 'visitation' looks like."* NCP Community *(on hiatus at the time of writing this book) is devoted to raising awareness of the issues faced by noncustodial parents; to combating stereotypes of noncustodial parents as irresponsible or even dangerous "deadbeats" who don't want their children; and to offering strategies and solutions that help all involved work together for the good of their children.*

In 2008, an MSN Living article (Bamberger 2008) named Spicuglia one of eight "Moms Inspired to Change History." In the e-mail interview below, originally posted on our blog (Philyaw and Thomas 2009), she challenges parents to rethink their definition of "noncustodial."

One of your goals in creating NCP Community was to raise awareness about the issues noncustodial parents face. What are some of the key issues?

Noncustodial parents face many of the same challenges that custodial parents face. We want to instill our values in our children, ensure they are doing their homework and studying for that big test tomorrow, treating others with respect. But it is much harder to do when you aren't in the same house as your children.

Parental disagreements are common, and a noncustodial parent can often feel helpless in decisions ranging from whether or not a child should have a cell phone to medical care [decisions]. But once you get past divorce and mediation issues and settle into everyday life, it's engaging our children's teachers, maintaining regular communication with our children, and arranging visitation that are the big issues. Visitation in particular can be very difficult. There is scheduling with the custodial parent, figuring out child care, trying to arrange playdates when you may not have much of a parenting community to speak of, and trying to make those visits really meaningful for our relationship with our children.

Yet, despite our best efforts and loving intentions, noncustodial parents often feel shut out from our children's day-to-day life, academic progress, and major decisions. In extreme cases, there might even be concern about the child's well-being, even child abuse, in the custodial parent's home. Societal misconceptions about what "noncustodial" means can wrongly limit a parent's access to their children's education or medical records, and parents often do not have access to legal resources or even understand their parental rights. This can be discouraging for a parent who is truly striving to do the best she or he can.

What are some common misconceptions about noncustodial parents?

One of the biggest issues noncustodial parents face is a lack of understanding generally in society about what "noncustodial" means. This leads to a great deal of frustration when dealing with authorities, and we regularly find ourselves explaining legalities to people to defend our right to be involved, our right to parent.

Just to clarify, there are two kinds of child custody—legal and physical—and there are varied combinations, which can even include a noncustodial parent sharing joint legal *and* physical custody. I do not have physical custody, but I share joint legal custody with my son's father, which gives me full parental authority under the law. But someone has to move out of the house, right? Every divorce naturally creates custodial and noncustodial parents, but the stereotypes of the deadbeat dad and disappearing mom leave a stigma that noncustodial parents are irresponsible or don't want their children, or worse—that they are dangerous and should be viewed with suspicion. In fact, the majority of noncustodial parents are law-abiding citizens and loving parents who want to be involved as much as possible in our children's lives.

On your blog, you posted a *Globe and Mail* article about "parental alienation syndrome" that noted: "Court proceedings are not conducive to peacemaking; they tend to increase acrimony between parents, which is bad for children. Many noncustodial parents simply walk away from an impossible situation, devastated to lose contact with their children, but consoled to know that their children's exposure to a toxic tug-of-war is over." What support is available to parents in these situations? What resources can they find at *NCP Community* or elsewhere?

What I loved about that article was the focus on the best interest of the child, which often gets lost in discussions of parental alienation syndrome. Sadly, many of us have seen how a parent might bad-mouth or poison a child against the other parent. Whether or not people agree on the definition of "parental alienation" or that PAS exists as a "syndrome," few people would disagree that the problem exists. Even if both parents have legal custody, the custodial parent is in a position of greater power than the noncustodial parent. It is much easier to interfere with visitation as the custodial parent. It is unfortunate that withholding visitation is a tactic often used, but when was the last time you saw an Amber Alert for "child abducted by custodial parent"?

Ideally, parents should be able to find ways to work together to prevent or manage these negative situations by bringing in mediators or planning ahead and building in very specific parenting plans into their custody agreements to prevent disputes. However, if the situation is very bad, legal counsel may be needed. NCPC is a place for sharing strategies and solutions that will help everyone work together for the best interest of our children.

What are some of the unique challenges for co-parents who live a far distance from their children? What are some ways they "stay close" when they don't live close by?

There are many reasons a parent might live far away from his or her child—living near family, finding work, or to start a new life—and while it is hard, families can make it work. In fact, it has become easier to keep in touch long-distance, with visitation via Skype and flying our kids unaccompanied to visit us.

Most important, no matter the distance, children should be able to continue the same quality of relationship with each parent that they enjoyed prior to the separation. Here are some suggestions for noncustodial parents:

- Regular phone calls, scheduled and unscheduled, help keep the lines of communication open and ensure that you are kept in the loop of your children's lives.

- In conversation, ask specific questions to show that you care and are paying attention. I find that those are easier questions for children to answer ("How did you do on your test?" versus "How was school today?")

- Be creative in your communications and demonstration of your love. Text messages, e-mails, cards, care packages....

Keep a stack of cute cards at the ready to send. Buy things that remind your children how special they are (magnets, pictures, ID-sized notes to fit into a wallet).

+ Communicate with the custodial parent. Again, the more specific the questions, the better. The custodial parent is a gold mine of information about your child and main decision-maker in your child's life, so open communication should always be a priority.

+ Don't be discouraged. Keep trying, and try not to place the burden of your frustration onto your children. Remember that despite the challenges you face, you are ultimately responsible for your involvement in your children's lives.

You've noted the growing voice of noncustodial mothers, particularly in social media. What are some special concerns that noncustodial moms face that noncustodial dads do not (or do to a lesser degree)?

Society can be harsh toward moms who don't fit a traditional mold. The assumption that [a mother] will retain custody of her children after a divorce is so strong that if she does not take custody, her fitness or attachment to her child comes into question in a way that it does not for men. People wonder if she had her children taken away from her, or maybe she just didn't want her kids. These are assumptions that often have no basis in reality. It may come down to which parent has more resources to offer the children, or which parent has the better lawyer.

What's most important is that custody arrangements are made in the best interest of the children, and although a child might reside with one parent, that should not reflect badly on the noncustodial mom or dad. At the end of the day, noncustodial moms and dads have more in common than not. We are just trying to stay involved in our children's lives in meaningful ways.

A Word to Custodial Parents

Imagine for a moment that the tables were turned. What if it was *your* job that took you out of state? What if, despite your efforts, the judge had awarded your ex primary custody? What if you went weeks or months at a time without seeing your child? What kind of access and interaction would you want in the interim? How often would you want to communicate? Would you want that communication supervised and monitored by the other parent? Would you want to know about milestones and school successes and so forth in a timely fashion? Would you want the privilege of congratulating and celebrating with your child, even from afar?

"People talk about deadbeat dads all the time in the media," says Robert, a noncustodial parent who lives several states away from his two sons. "Guys who could be with their kids but who choose not to. But what you don't hear about is guys like me who *want* to be with our kids, but have to deal with an ex in another state who constantly blocks access, in violation of court orders. It's killing me, it's killing my relationship with my kids, and they are hurting too. But let my ex tell it, the kids don't want to see me and this is my punishment for divorcing her."

Are you supporting and encouraging your child's relationship with the other parent the way you'd want *her* to if *you* were the noncustodial parent? Some co-parents say, "Well, if I left town then I wouldn't deserve to have equal status and all those perks as a parent." Or, "If I cheated and my spouse left town with the kids and I never saw them, then I'd be getting what I deserved." Leaving aside the legal fallacies in those statements, those parents should consider: *What does my child deserve? What does* she *want?* Disregarding any outside suggestions that a noncustodial parent is less of a parent, less interested in the child, or less worthy, it's also important to consider: *What does my child really want? What is she entitled to?*

If you are co-parenting with a noncustodial parent, we encourage you to revisit the Children's Bill of Rights in chapter 1. Do your actions consistently honor your child's rights to a secure, caring relationship with the other parent? Even if you believe the other parent is dropping the ball in some areas, are you making *your* best effort in this regard?

A Happy Ending

A noncustodial mom who blogs under the name Sophia Van Buren shared some reflections about her parenting journey with us. Custodial as well as noncustodial parents can learn much from Van Buren's hard-won wisdom (personal communication, Nov. 17, 2011):

> When I am stressed out or frustrated, wondering, like I often do, if I am doing the right thing for my children, I just look at them and a sense of calm washes over me. They are all turning out well. Really well, in fact.
>
> The other day, [my daughter] Claire and I were hanging out, relaxing, catching up, and talking about what she might want to do with her future. College, friendship, dating, driving, part-time job, fashion... My oldest daughter is now seventeen. She's figuring out the world on her own, little by little. One thing that has turned out to be a real benefit to being an Every Other Weekend parent is that when I spend time with my kids, we seem to know how precious it is, and we are fully engaged. We talk about meaningful things, important life subjects. Claire even asks my opinion every once in a while, and when I give it to her, she actually seems to listen. At least sometimes, I am not just white noise to my teen daughter.
>
> Claire is wise beyond her years, and she is heading in the right direction. I've worried about how divorce has tainted my children's lives. I fretted that by not waging a legal battle and allowing myself to become a noncustodial mother, I've damaged them somehow, or done something wrong even though it seemed the best option for my kids at the time. But I think I've done some things right, too. By putting your kids first, especially during times of trial and stress, you

make choices that may be difficult, but that can end up making them into better people in the long run.

Our friend Fritz put it perfectly over the summer when I confided to him that I regularly worried that letting their father have physical custody of them without a fight was a big mistake. Claire was at the tail end of a five-week nannying stint for Fritz's young family with three children in Europe. I valued this man's opinion and listened closely when he offered it. He's an intelligent and successful auto executive in Europe and had come to know my daughter well. She'd lived with the five of them at home and on travels to Hungary, Austria, and Germany. Fritz was extremely impressed with Claire's work ethic, her positive attitude, and the intelligent way she conducted herself. He reminded me of how "together" my Claire is, and what an unusually resilient person she's evolved into as a young woman.

"Sophia, think of a pearl," he started out. "It is beautiful and valuable and rare because of all the irritation that it endures. That irritation is exactly what creates it. I really think that environment is a big reason why Claire is so mature. She hasn't had it easy, but it's made her into a strong person."

Chances are, Claire would be the same Claire had I remained a stay-at-home mom. I'd never know. But maybe there was some truth to what Fritz had said.

It hasn't been easy, but my Claire is now as strong, well-rounded, and beautiful as a gleaming pearl. Perhaps not in spite of how things in our life have gone, but *because* of it.

Parental Reinvolvement

When a parent who has been absent from a child's life returns and wants to be actively involved again, or for the first time, the process of reinvolvement (sometimes called reengagement) has many steps. First, if the parents were never married, and the parent who seeks to reengage is the father, paternity must be officially established before he can exercise any of his paternal rights. Even if the parents were previously married or the parental rights were otherwise previously established, an extended absence from a child's life may warrant a reconsideration of any earlier parenting time schedule. Simply put, it's not good for kids to have a parent be in and out of their lives; children need consistency and they need to be able to rely on the adults who are responsible for their care. Children and parents need support, particularly in the form of family counseling, to make this transition. A court may mandate a period of supervised time for parent-child reacquaintance before resumption of a regular parenting time schedule.

The key to successful parental reinvolvement is the custodial parent. This parent, who has borne all the responsibility in the other parent's absence, not only controls access to the child, but also sets the emotional tone surrounding reengagement. Will the custodial parent allow her understandable sadness, reluctance, resentment, or fear to influence her to discourage the reunion? Or will she do the tough job of working through and managing those emotions, in order to allow her child the opportunity to have a relationship with the other parent? How do you balance the very real need to protect a child from a parent who previously failed to act in the child's best interest with the parent and child's right to have a relationship with each other? This balancing act is the reason courts and therapists prescribe that reengagement be a gradual, monitored process.

For more tips on how to create a solid partnership as a noncustodial parent, or *with* a noncustodial parent, revisit chapter 7. In the next chapter, we'll look at a co-parenting milestone that challenges custodial and noncustodial parents alike: the introduction of a new significant other to the children.

Part III

"But You Don't Know My Ex"

For the sake of children in divorced families everywhere, we wish that all parents could co-parent "by the book," adhering perfectly to all the advice in the previous sections. But our own co-parenting journey doesn't even meet those criteria. We've certainly had our share of bumps in the road. This section offers guidance and encouragement for navigating those inevitable bumps, including specific advice for those who are struggling to co-parent under difficult circumstances. We answer questions such as: What if your ex insists on being uncooperative? What if your ex struggles with mental health or substance abuse issues? How do you co-parent after domestic violence?

And we'll discuss one potential bump that affects many parenting partnerships: the introduction of a new significant other.

Chapter 11

Co-parenting, Dating, and Remarriage

Remarriage is an excellent test of just how
amicable your divorce was.

—Margo Kaufman

It's an all-too-common co-parenting story: "My ex and I were getting along just great, parenting the kids together, no drama. Then I started dating...and all hell broke loose."

What is it about dating and remarriage that can cause a previously civil or even friendly parenting partnership to run off the rails? Here are some of the "Everything was fine, until..." scenarios that co-parents have shared with us:

- "My son hasn't come to my house since his mother found out about my girlfriend. She told me that she didn't want him around my girlfriend and won't let me take him even if I tell her that my girlfriend isn't going to be at my house while he's there. She's upset because she wants to get back together and I don't. I am taking her to court for this, but in the meantime, she's making my life and my son's life hell."

+ "The day after we mailed our wedding invitations, my ex-wife filed to increase the amount of child support I pay her. Not only am I already paying her more than the law requires, but she had congratulated me on my engagement!"

+ "My ex-girlfriend allows our three-year-old daughter to share a bed with her and her boyfriend. I tried to talk to her about it, but she thinks I'm just jealous. Then her boyfriend threatened me."

+ "My daughter came home and told me that her father and his new wife insist that she call this woman 'Mom.' I was livid."

+ "My ex told our kids that they don't have to respect their stepmother. Our house has turned into a war zone."

When a co-parent begins dating or remarries, several lives and relationships are put to the test. The idea of one's ex being close to someone else can irritate the still-fresh or newly healed wounds from the divorce. Parents may, wittingly or unwittingly, pressure their kids to declare loyalty to them by rejecting the other parent's new partner. They may also fear that the new significant other will usurp their role as a parent or take away from the time, money, and other resources their children are entitled to from the dating parent. The dating or remarried parent's new relationship also flies in the face of any reconciliation fantasy the other parent or the child may have.

Children who are used to having their parent's undivided time and attention must now face the prospect of sharing. They may also fear that acceptance of the new partner will be seen as a betrayal of the other parent.

Lovestruck, the dating parent may, wittingly or unwittingly, rush his child into accepting this new person in her life too deeply and too soon. This parent may also feel an unwinnable tug-of-war between parenting demands and relationship demands.

Finally, the new partner has to navigate life with the co-parent's child even as the new couple is still building their relationship. Congeniality between co-parents, which is best for the child, may be the very thing that unsettles the new partner. A fearful or insecure partner may push the co-parent to grant her access to his children sooner than he'd like to, in order to prove his commitment to the relationship. Hoping to avoid a conflict with his partner, the co-parent acquiesces...only to end up in conflict with his ex or his children or both, as a result.

So, one lesson many dating and remarried co-parents learn is this: You can't please everyone all the time. You can, however, do your best to be thoughtful and patient with the process and with each other, starting with the introduction.

Our Story

When Mike and Deesha began dating the people who later became our spouses, it felt like a long game of secret agent. We didn't hide the fact that we were dating from each other, but we did hide some aspects of our dating lives from our children. In some instances, they were aware that we dated, but they never saw us on a date. That's where the secret agent activity came into play. When one or both of us would go out, we stayed in communication with each other regarding our whereabouts in order to avoid running into the kids while in the company of someone new to them. We didn't want the kids to meet anyone we were dating until we were as sure as we could be that this was someone with whom we wanted to make a serious commitment.

After a period of dating our future spouses—one year for Deesha, and three years for Mike—we each decided that we were ready for our kids to meet the special person in our lives. We gave the other parent the opportunity to meet this new person first. After these meetings, our children were gradually introduced, starting with brief outings in public places with our "special friends," working up to more involved interactions and the children's full awareness that we were dating.

The above sums up what we decided was best for our family with regard to dating with kids in the mix, what Yvonne Kelly—stepfamily coach, counselor, and founder of the Step and Blended Family Institute—calls step-dating. You may decide that different terms work for you and your kids. If you and your ex can agree on these terms, that's a bonus for your kids and will help ensure that your parenting partnership survives the journey through this new terrain intact. Below you'll find strategies and advice for dating that we've gleaned from our own experiences and those of other co-parents who have taken this step into a new chapter of their lives. Consider what works for and what applies to you and your family.

Don't Date

It's an ironic piece of advice to give a co-parent who wants to date, but many experts and veteran co-parents agree: Don't rush into dating. Give yourself an opportunity to decompress, learn, and grow on your own after your relationship with your co-parent ends. Maybe you've never lived on your own, or maybe it's been a while. Enjoy having time to think about nothing but your own needs and your kids'. Taking a break between relationships gives you the opportunity to reflect on issues in your previous relationship—what some call your baggage—in the hopes that you won't face the same challenges in your next relationship. Learning about yourself, what you want in a partner, and what you have to offer a partner and deciding on the kind of relationship you want is vital.

"I don't want to pay for the last guy's mistakes," says Reggie, a divorced dad of an eleven-year-old boy. "I took the time to work on *me* after my divorce, mentally, physically, and emotionally, and I want a partner who has done the same. I'm in a much better place to offer someone a healthy relationship, and in the end that's not only good for me and good for her, but good for my son, to see a healthy relationship."

Timing Is Everything

Even though we use the term "step-dating," of course not everyone you date will be a serious contender to be your child's stepparent. But the term does imply something significant: your dating practices as they relate to your kids will be part of the groundwork you lay for any future stepfamily you build. This is but one reason to be discerning when introducing your children to your dating partners.

Why Wait?

Safety is another reason. Just as, for your own safety, you take the time to get to know someone before you invite them to your home, visit their home, or ride in their car, you'll also want to control the access that others have to your child. In their parenting plans, some co-parents include a provision agreeing to the minimum amount of dating time required—six months is common—before a child may be introduced to a new partner. The provision may also state that overnight guests are not allowed when the child is present.

Another consideration is how much time has passed since the divorce or separation. You and your new partner may feel as if you're ready for introductions to the kids, but if your child is not in a good place emotionally because the breakup is still fresh, or if he is having a particularly difficult time adjusting to specific changes like a new house or a new school, he'll probably be less receptive to this new person than he may be at a later time.

An additional reason for being discriminating about introductions is that you don't want your child to develop an attachment to someone you barely know and who may not be in your child's life in the long run. The pain of a breakup for you may be compounded for your child, who could experience this as yet another loss on top of the divorce. Having or seeing various grown-ups come into and go out of their lives and their parents' lives could leave children confused or jaded about the nature of commitment. It could lead them to the conclusion that relationships are fleeting because sooner or later, everyone leaves. Making healthy choices about your dating life can equip your child to make healthy choices about his in the future.

So when is the right time to introduce your kids to your new partner? The answer is the time that allows your kids the best chance at making a positive connection with a new partner whom you've vetted to the best of your ability. This doesn't mean your child has to be excited about this new person. A common misconception among co-parents is that if *they* are happy and in love with this person, their kids will automatically or quickly develop positive feelings toward him as well. Other common assumptions about introducing a new partner are:

+ *I enjoy spending time with him and think he's a lot of fun, so my kids will like being around him too.*

+ *Everyone will be happier if we go ahead and make the introductions because then I can spend more time with her and the kids, instead of waiting until they're at their dad's house.*

+ *It'll be great spending Thanksgiving with his kids and my kids all together.*

With visions of *The Brady Bunch* dancing in their heads, some co-parents see the introduction of two sets of kids as somehow easier because kids love to play with other kids, right? They do…but it gets complicated when those other kids have a parent attached. Introducing one set of kids at a time can help simplify things. Also, major holidays, birthdays, and other private occasions are not ideal times to make introductions to a new partner or a new partner's children. Having relative strangers included in such intimate celebrations can feel like an intrusion.

Think of the assumptions above as wishes. Such wishes are not guaranteed to come true, but, with patience on your part and a lot of listening to your child's feelings about this new development, eventually they may.

What's the Rush?

Contrary to everything we've just suggested, your child may be champing at the bit to meet the new person in your life. If you don't believe the time is right to make the introduction, but your child is curious about or interested in meeting someone you're dating, you can explain as Val did to her daughter: "I told her, 'You're so special to me that only really, really special people get to meet you. And it takes time to get to know someone to see just how special they are.'"

Even if your children are aware that you're dating, as ours were, and eager to meet new partners, don't be surprised by a change of heart—or several changes of heart—down the road. We've heard from several stepmoms that everything was great with their future stepkids—until the wedding. A wedding deals a serious blow to the parental reconciliation fantasy that many children have.

"Why Won't My Boyfriend Introduce Me to His Kids?"

Perhaps it's your new partner who's pressing you for an introduction to your children. One of the most common e-mails we receive from visitors to coparenting101.org isn't from co-parents at all; it's from women dating co-parenting dads, many of whom are frustrated or confused as to why their partner hasn't introduced them to his kids. They recognize what a big step this introduction is, so they seek it as a sign of a man's commitment. In the absence of an introduction, they question his commitment and ask how long they should remain invested in the relationship. Some have already introduced *their* children to the guy and believe he should follow suit. How do you respond to this, as a co-parent?

Your approach to dating and the limits you set in the best interest of your child may be difficult for your significant other to understand if she is not also a cooperative co-parent. She may find it difficult to accept that you and your ex have a prior agreement about how you'll handle introductions. She may have fears and insecurities about the relationship, including the fear that your co-parenting may lead you to rekindle things with your ex. Some co-parents walk the fine line between seeking to calm these fears while also communicating that their children are their priority. Not their *only* priority, but definitely not to be considered in competition with their significant other.

"I'm not proud of it, but I totally have moments where I felt jealous of my boyfriend's daughter," says Gennie, a divorced college professor with no kids. "The time he spends with her, the money he spends on her…she's his primary concern. I haven't even met her yet, and already it's been really hard. But I don't say any of this to him; I just deal with it. I'm also not thrilled about how chummy he is with his ex, his daughter's mom. I feel like his dirty little secret, while his daughter is the center of the universe. Then I come back to reality, and I remind myself that I'm thirty-four and she's nine. If anyone needs to take one for the team for a while it's me, not her."

Gennie was raised by a single father who dated several women before marrying Gennie's stepmother. She remembers, "I saw some of those women totally not getting that my brother and I were my father's priorities. They pushed for too much too fast in our lives, and so they didn't work out."

Let your new partner know that you want his future relationship with your child to have a fighting chance. So you're giving it the best start possible by being thoughtful—and patient—about the timing of the introduction. Your relationship with your new partner, your relationship with your kids, and the success of your possible stepfamily are all worth the wait.

Meet the Kids

Before introducing your kids to your new partner, we recommend a lot of communication among all involved—including your co-parent.

Talk about It...Before and After

It can be helpful for kids and for the parenting partnership if the other parent is made aware of the new relationship before any introductions are made. Telling your co-parent about this possible development in your child's life prevents her from feeling blindsided and prepares her to respond to your child's comments or concerns.

Some co-parents afford the other parent the opportunity to meet their new partner, either before or after the kids do; others don't. Some co-parents want to meet the new significant other; others don't. Some new partners want to meet the ex; others don't.

When telling your kids there's someone you'd like them to meet, make sure they know they are entitled to their feelings about this introduction, whatever those may be. Before and after you all spend time with your new partner, invite your child's questions and listen to what she has to say. Some kids may also need the reassurance that they will be given time and space to gradually get to know this new person, without pressure to like her immediately. Be sure that your expectations and your partner's expectations are aligned with what you tell your children in this regard.

In our family, from the introductions to the present day, we've reaffirmed our children's rights to their feelings—however mixed or uncomfortable—but we do expect them to show our new partners respect.

Introducing...

Public, short, and hopefully sweet. That's our suggestion for a good first meeting between your kids and your special someone. While you can control the circumstances of the meeting, don't worry if they don't hit it off that first time, or even in the near future. Give it time.

Some good first meeting spots co-parents have mentioned to us are parks, playgrounds, ice cream parlors, and pizza places. Keep it simple and enjoyable for the kids. If the kids are doing something they like, this can help the introductions along.

Even if you introduce your partner as a "friend," your child's growing awareness may prompt questions about the nature of your relationship. Regardless of how you present it, seeing you with someone else can trigger your child's thoughts about the other parent and the fantasy he may have about you reuniting. Your child may also be reluctant to share your time and attention with someone else. These and other issues may come up in your subsequent conversations with your child about your new partner, or you may see behavior that suggests your child is struggling to adapt. Continue to listen to your child and to reassure her of her unique place in your life.

After Mike's wife, Sherry, met our daughters for the first time, she sent Deesha a text message thanking her for the opportunity to get to know the girls. Of course Sherry didn't need Deesha's permission to meet our daughters, but she believes Deesha's positive attitude toward her freed the girls to get to know her. Deesha paid it forward by sending a similar text to her husband's ex, after meeting their kids for the first time.

Unfortunately for some children, a parent may respond to news of the new partner by interfering with the dating parent's parenting time. If your co-parent resists having your child interact with your new partner for unfounded reasons, it may be necessary to pursue legal measures to ensure that your parenting time is honored consistently. Also, family counseling can help children navigate their own feelings about the new partner and deal with any confusion or fear related to the parental conflict.

The Fear Factor

A common co-parenting stereotype is that of the angry ex. When a co-parent begins dating or remarries, a previously civil ex can turn into an angry ex, or an already angry ex can turn into an even angrier one. But remember what a wise man (okay, Yoda) once said about anger: "Fear leads to anger." What if you could look beneath your ex's anger (or look beneath your own anger, if it's your co-parent who's dating or has remarried) and see her fear instead? It might look like one or more of the following:

I'm afraid that my ex's new partner will try to replace me as a parent.

I'm afraid that I am inadequate as a parent and that my children will enjoy being with my ex and her spouse more than they enjoy being with me.

I'm afraid of my own feelings about my ex's new partner...I thought I was over him, so why do I feel jealous and resentful?

I'm afraid that I'm less worthy and less desirable than my ex's new wife. He never treated me as well as he treats her. He never took me to the places he takes her.

I'm afraid that my children and other people will compare me to my ex's new partner and find me lacking.

I'm afraid that my ex will have misplaced priorities and become an irresponsible parent now that he's with someone else.

I'm afraid that my ex's spouse will try to make changes in our parenting plan.

I'm afraid that my ex's spouse will mistreat our child.

I'm afraid that my ex will limit our communication and interactions now.

I'm afraid that my ex and I will never get back together now that's she's seeing someone else.

Of the fears above, are there any that you can address for your co-parent, offering reassurance? Telling your co-parent that she can never be replaced as a parent could go a long way toward helping her adjust to your new partner's involvement in your children's lives. Of course, some of the fears have to do with boundary issues and your co-parent's personal healing process; in this case, stay positive, and give her time and space to adjust.

Adhering to your parenting plan may also help minimize conflict while everyone adjusts to your new relationship. Remember that while flexibility is important, your ex is under no obligation to swap times to accommodate your dating life or your spouse's schedule. Try to schedule your personal plans for times when the kids aren't with you, or be prepared to hire a sitter if your co-parent won't swap.

If Your Co-Parent Is Dating or Has Remarried

If your co-parent has begun to date or has remarried, do any of the fears in the above section sound familiar? If so, consider ways to confront the fears and boost your confidence, without burdening your children or your ex. You might find it helpful to revisit chapter 2 for suggestions for continuing the healing and grieving process.

Respecting boundaries is at the heart of any successful parenting partnership. Now that your co-parent is in another relationship, those boundaries should remain intact. While you can't dictate the terms of your ex's new relationship, you may request (or accept) an opportunity to meet the new partner. Perhaps this meeting and an honest conversation with your ex about your concerns will help calm your fears.

New partners can easily become whipping boys and girls for rocky co-parenting situations. If your ex is late for drop-offs or pick-ups, or is otherwise dropping the co-parenting ball, resist the urge to blame the new partner. Regardless of the new partner's presence or participation, the only person with an obligation to you and your children is your co-parent. The new partner can't do anything that your co-parent doesn't allow, so be sure to take your concerns or complaints directly to your ex.

Give Your Child Permission

If you can't be enthusiastic about your child connecting well with the new partner, at least be neutral about it. "I didn't expect my ex to turn cartwheels after my kids and I went to Disney World with my girlfriend," said Evan, a dad of three. "But I totally wasn't prepared for what she did. When my oldest son started telling her about our trip, she forbid them to say my name, my girlfriend's name, or even 'Disney World,' in her house ever again. Totally ridiculous." After that, Evan noticed that his children were reluctant to be around his girlfriend. Things got worse once the couple married. Evan's children, conflicted, felt obligated to honor their mother by holding their stepmother at arm's length.

Maybe your parting salvo to your co-parent before you separated was a vow that you'd never allow your child to interact with any new partner he may have—or with a specific partner, in the case of an affair. You'll need to work through the anger and hurt that led you to make that declaration, so that you can avoid disrupting your ex's parenting time or making your child feel conflicted about something over which she has no control.

If, however, you truly believe the new partner poses a serious threat to your children's well-being and your ex won't address the issue, use the legal and therapeutic resources available to you to protect your children.

Short of that, respect your co-parent's right to date, remarry, and move on with her life. This includes her right to be accompanied by her partner to public events such as your child's soccer game or school performances, when the time is right, without fear of an ugly scene that will upset your child. Free your child from the fear that you will consider him disloyal or otherwise be upset or hurt if he shows willingness to accept the new partner. Give him permission to continue loving and spending time with both parents, unconditionally.

Avoid Giving the Third Degree

While showing interest when your children talk about their time with the other parent is always a positive, be careful that the conversation doesn't become an interrogation about Mom or Dad's new significant other. The difference between showing interest and interrogating is subtle and has to do with your intentions. The former lets your child know that it's okay for her to have a relationship with the other parent and this new person and to talk with you about it; the latter serves to satisfy your curiosity and to put your child on notice that you're not okay with the new partner.

Moving On

For some co-parents, their ex's new relationship or remarriage deals a final, unwelcome blow to a reconciliation fantasy. The good news is this development may be the catalyst these co-parents need to finally move on with their lives.

For your co-parent, moving on may include remarriage.

Joining Families: You Don't Need a Blender

As with all aspects of co-parenting, communicating with your children is of utmost importance when sharing your decision to marry. "You don't know what it's going to be like for children to hear their father is getting married," says Anthony, a politician and remarried co-parenting father of two. "You want to make sure you do it in a way that's sensitive to their needs and emotions."

And after the wedding ceremony, the need for sensitivity remains as everyone works to adapt to the new family structure. "I'm not fond of the term 'blended families,'" says Bari Benjamin, a psychotherapist, licensed clinical social worker, mother, and stepmother. "'Blended' can sometimes give adults and children unreasonable expectations about adjusting to stepfamily life" (personal communication, June 2009). When a co-parent and a new partner decide to form a family unit, it takes time. Love shared between the grown-ups does not mean that love will reign quickly, if at all, among the children toward each other and toward the adults.

Unfortunately, the odds are stacked against remarriages with children. Remarriages with children experience a 50 percent higher divorce rate than those without children, according to Wednesday Martin (2009), author of *Stepmonster*. Also, more than half of all adult women in the United States will marry a man with children at some point in their lives, and up to 70 percent of those unions will end. Clearly, having children in the mix poses a challenge to marriages. Some stepparents and remarried co-parents have observed that their kids felt differently—less excited, sad, or even suddenly angry and disagreeable—as the wedding day approached or after the wedding. Honest, ongoing communication is a vital part of weathering these storms, as well as the storms to come in daily life together. Mike has found that a weekly or monthly family meeting has helped him, his wife, and our children address concerns that come up in their household.

We can both attest to the fact that even with patience and the help of proactive, honest communication, certain parts of your family will, in many ways, remain distinct and not blend. For a variety of reasons, some bonds and relationships will be closer than others. And that's okay. From the outset, to remove the pressure to bond and love each other instantly, Deesha and her husband had one rule for their collective four daughters: *everyone just has to feel comfortable, safe, and respected.* They believe it's precisely this low-pressure approach that has created the loving bonds they and their stepchildren share today.

Also, your co-parent's influence will be felt in your stepfamily, for better or for worse. Hopefully, your parenting partnership will facilitate and not hinder your efforts to grow as a stepfamily. But even this best-case scenario can have its challenges. According to Yvonne Kelly of the Step and Blended Family Institute, whether you have a rocky or a rosy co-parenting relationship, a new spouse might resent it. "The working together of the exes," she says, "can be perceived and experienced as threatening or at least downright annoying to the new person" (personal communication, May 18, 2009). To some extent, the problem is one of insecurity on the part of the stepparent, in the face of the closeness of the former partners as co-parents. However, part of the problem is also the inability of the stepparent—and perhaps other members of the family as well—to see how the step-parent fits into the family equation. If taking care of the children is already going so smoothly, where does a stepmother fit in? What role can a stepfather play?

Conversely, when the former couple is at odds, the stepparent knows exactly where she fits in. Says Kelly (ibid.), "The new couple, in this case, is more solid and united in their 'war,' for lack of a better word, with the ex. This isn't necessarily the healthiest way for a couple to bond—over their mutual dislike of the [former spouse], but it sets up boundaries that do work at some level for the new couple."

Stepparents need the reassurance that cooperative parenting after divorce is indeed a good thing that will ultimately benefit every-one. But they also need the validation and recognition of their place in their household and in their spouse's life.

Stepfamily Survival Toolbox

Given the above challenges, we believe that every stepfamily can benefit from having a "survival toolbox" that contains the following six essentials:

1. Patience

2. Respect

3. Reasonable expectations of themselves and each other

4. Clearly articulated roles (A stepparent's primary role is to support her spouse in the parenting role, even if they don't

always agree with regard to parenting decisions. This support takes different forms in different families, but the distinction should be made clear.)

5. Honest communication

6. Help when needed—in the form of counseling, taking a break, and comforting each other

Whole-Family Events

Since our separation and subsequent divorce, we've made a point of sitting together at our children's school and sporting events whenever possible and enjoying occasional meals and other outings together with our children. Now that we're both remarried, our whole family—children, spouses, and stepchildren—socializes from time to time and goes on annual vacation. In *The Family Dinner: Great Ways to Connect with Your Kids, One Meal at a Time*, TV and film producer and author Laurie David explains the importance of continuing to connect in this way after divorce (David and Uhrenholdt 2010):

Today half of all marriages end in divorce. That's an awful lot of family dinners in jeopardy. It's unfortunate that just as kids need rituals most, when they are the most fragile and insecure, a great stabilizer like family dinner is often the first thing to go. Lots of factors contribute to this: the pain of the empty seat (no one wants to sit there, and if they did they would regret it when the reprimand came: "But that's Dad's seat!"); the emotional wreckage of the remaining parent; the sadness of the kids, often masked by sullenness; the convenient mindless tempting escape of the television…the list is endless.

When marriages break up, kids need the comfort of routine more than ever. When life is suddenly unpredictable and scary, rituals come to the rescue doing what they do best, providing a sense of predictability and normalcy, stability and security, comfort and love.

I speak from personal experience. All the rituals I had spent years establishing helped me and my kids enormously, and [my ex-husband] Larry, too. Continuing them sent the message loud and clear that although our family was changing, life would go on, routines would continue, dinner would be served.

When considering whole-family events—with or without new spouses—keep the following in mind:

- These events affirm that kids are still part of a loving family, albeit now divided into two households.

- Communication and planning are essential.

- Although initially your kids may love these get-togethers, you should check in with them periodically to see whether this holds true over time.

- Whole-family events can feed a reconciliation fantasy.

- Whole-family events can be a wonderful gift to your children, but not if there is unmanageable conflict in the co-parenting or stepfamily dynamic.

This chapter offered a blueprint of sorts for navigating dating and remarriage. Having a game plan increases your chance of success in these and other aspects of co-parenting. However, even the best-laid plans can go up in flames if an uncooperative ex is determined to torch them. In the next chapter, we'll look at fifteen things you can do in spite of your ex's unwillingness to cooperate, if this is a problem for you.

Chapter 12

Fifteen Things You Can Do for Your Child in Spite of Your Uncooperative Ex

I doubt my ex and I will ever be cordial. However, I do continue to try. By doing so, we can teach our daughters how to better handle people who frustrate them.

—Lara

In this chapter, we'll address the hard cases, the tough nuts to crack, the brick walls…you get the idea. When you've tried to communicate and cooperate with your ex to no avail, or when substance abuse, mental illness, or domestic violence is a factor in your co-parenting situation, you may feel powerless to protect your children from the emotional distress and other consequences related to your ex's behavior. But the good news is you can still make a positive difference in your children's lives. Your children are worth your best effort regardless of what the other parent does or does not do. So here we present fifteen things you can do for your child that do not require your ex's cooperation.

1. Declare Your House a Peaceful Zone

Commit to making your house and your parenting time a safe, peaceful haven for your child. Refuse to engage in arguments with your ex (either in person or on the phone) when your child is present. Keep conversations with your child centered on your child's interest and well-being and other topics—not your ex's negativity.

2. Accept That Your Co-Parent May Never Change

A big step toward achieving personal peace is accepting that your high-conflict co-parent may not change her ways. Pedro, a father of three, told us, "I drove myself nuts trying to find just the right book, the perfect blog, the perfect inspirational quote to make my ex-wife want to get along...or at least feel remorse for how she was treating our kids and me. Nothing helped. After a few years of that, I decided to just focus on being the best parent that I can be, the parent my kids deserve, regardless of what their mother does."

Accept that your ex may never change. Then, if at some point your ex does become more cooperative, you'll be happily surprised.

3. Affirm Your Child without Bad-Mouthing Your Ex

Refuse to respond to negative comments from your ex. Model for your child how to be the "bigger" person. Your child may ask you about the other parent's bad-mouthing. You can tell her that while it is wrong and hurtful to say such things, the most important thing to you is taking care of her and spending time with her. Reassure her that *she*, rather than your ex's words, is your focus. If the other parent's bad-mouthing is a source of stress and concern for your child, seek the help of a family counselor.

4. Try Not to Take It Personally

Here's a story from one co-parenting mom: "I found a text message in my daughter's phone from her father, who is mostly absent from her life, by choice. The message said, 'I would spend more time with you and call you more...but I hate your mother.' My daughter is nine. In what universe is that even remotely appropriate to say to a child? And I definitely brought it up the next time we went to court, and the judge got on his case about it. But beyond that, those words really hurt. I had to remind myself that he's entitled to his opinion, and I'm free to ignore it."

It's hard to ignore your ex's vitriol. But try not to take hateful words to heart, and don't make your ex's problems your problem. There's a saying: *what other people think about you is none of your business.*

5. Filter Your Ex's Communications: Taneshia's Story

"I finally realized that the problems in my co-parenting situation weren't all the ridiculous things my ex would accuse me of in his daily abusive e-mail rants to me. The problem was those e-mails," says Taneshia. "I read them in part because I was afraid that if I ignored them, I might miss something actually relevant, like a schedule change. But I think I also read them because I was just so used to that dynamic between my ex and me: he would rant, and then I would go on the defensive and rant back. It really bothered me that he considers me a bad mother. So even when I didn't respond to the e-mails, I kept reading them because this was a dance I'd done with him for years, and they were daily affirmation of what a horrible person he is."

Taneshia continued this draining dance until her best friend got tired of hearing her complain about the e-mails. "She said, 'If you're serious about moving on with your life, you'll stop reading those e-mails.' She suggested that I change e-mail addresses and only use the old account to communicate with him. Then I agreed to let her lock me out of that account by changing the password, because I didn't have the willpower at first to stop reading the e-mails. Once a week, she would tell me if there was anything in the e-mails from him that actually warranted a response, and if so, I'd send her the response and she'd forward it to him from my old account.

"In the first month of doing this, she sent only one response. I felt like a weight had been lifted. After a few months, I had my friend unlock the old account. Even with access, I found that I'd lost the desire to read his rants word for word. After about a year, when I resumed responsibility for communicating with him, I felt so wonderfully detached. I have developed my own internal filter that allows me to bypass all the nastiness in the e-mail and quickly determine if there's anything important pertaining to our child. I typically limit my responses to him to one e-mail per week, if I respond at all."

6. Laugh to Keep from Crying

Sometimes, the dynamics of a co-parenting situation are so over the top that a parent can't help but laugh at the outrageousness of it all. Being able to find the humor in stressful and upsetting moments is a skill that, unfortunately, some co-parents have numerous opportunities to cultivate. Here are two funny stories co-parents have shared with us:

> My ex reminds me of Wile E. Coyote, always trying to blow up the Roadrunner (that's me) or drop heavy objects on him. And all of his schemes backfire, and while he ends up burned to a crisp or flattened or falling off the edge of a cliff, the Roadrunner just keeps speeding past, oblivious, not even acknowledging him. *I'm not oblivious to my ex's anger, but I don't let it destroy me either.*
>
> [One night] I spent half the night in the emergency room with my son, Kieran, and my ex, Seamus. Kieran returned from an international trip with infections in both feet. I was a little annoyed with Seamus because I wanted to take Kieran to an urgent care practice through my insurance, Kaiser, which would be faster and cheaper. Plus, they have all his medical records. But Seamus knows just how to defuse me, crack a joke and make me laugh. Hours later, we were still in the waiting room, and Seamus and Kieran were both saying, "I have a great idea. Next time, let's just go to Kaiser!" So we actually had a pretty good time together playing silly little games like guessing why others were at the ER, and I have to say we were the only ones in the emergency room laughing. Which reminded me: attitude really is so much of the equation. We have challenges, like sick children and co-parenting with somebody we used to love, and we can approach these realities [either] with humor and an adventurous spirit, or with a sullen, bitter attitude.

This story is our favorite:

At this point, things were admittedly uncomfortable. My ex-husband had no visitation and there was a temporary restraining order in place. So it's Father's Day, and a guy in an Elmo suit shows up on our porch totally unannounced, 9 a.m. on a Sunday. So we try to ignore the doorbell, hoping the guy will go away, and then Elmo starts pounding on the door. So…guy in a face-obscuring mask, aggressively and angrily pounding on the door… must be the ex, right? So we call the police.

An officer shows up and demands that "Elmo" verify his identity. And "Elmo" makes the unfortunate, but retroactively hilarious, choice to stay in character.

Officer: I need to see some ID.

Elmo: Elmo no have ID.

Officer: You need to take that head off and show me your face.

Elmo: No take Elmo's head off!

Officer: Knock it off. I'm serious. Take the head off, or you're going to jail.

"Elmo" finally gets that it's not a joke and takes his head off. And it's some poor bastard the ex hired, without notifying us that an Elmo impersonator would be showing up at 9 a.m. Sunday morning, and without telling this guy about the custody situation. So this poor guy gets the cops called on him and almost hauled off to jail because he got played.

By the way, the pounding on the door was the result of a trying-to-be-helpful neighbor telling "Elmo": "I know they're there. They just must not hear you."

Postscript: "Elmo" gets ready to leave, puts his head back on, walks off the porch to the front sidewalk, sighs, hangs his head, and says (back in character): "Elmo sad!" And then shuffles off.

7. Refrain from Diagnosing Your Ex

If you suspect that your ex is suffering from a mental illness or addiction to a substance, address specific problem behaviors as they relate to your children, without trying to diagnose. Mental illness or substance abuse does not automatically negate her right to parent, so contact an attorney or your local family court to learn how to proceed. While co-parents shouldn't invest themselves in trying to diagnose their exes, understanding more about addiction or specific illnesses could be useful.

8. Request Conditional Parenting Time

Some co-parents' parenting time is supervised or otherwise conditional because of mental health, substance abuse, or domestic violence issues. Despite these issues, they may still be able to exercise parental rights and their children may still desire a relationship with them. That said, co-parenting should never put a child or parent in harm's way.

For Tracey, being a gatekeeper has been necessary to protect her child after incidents of domestic violence perpetrated by her ex-husband. "I attended the court-ordered co-parenting classes, and they stressed how important it is for children to have both parents in their lives, and how it hurts kids if one parent keeps them from the other. So when my ex accused me of keeping our son from him, it was like a knife in the heart. I felt so guilty. But he doesn't attend the anger management classes and drug counseling that the judge ordered, and he refuses to have supervised visits. He just wants me to let him come and pick up our son. But I just can't do it."

Parenting is not an absolute right, but parents do have an absolute responsibility to act in their children's best interest. When mental health or other issues hinder a parent's ability to do so, parenting time may be contingent upon attending anger management classes, completing a rehabilitation program, or fulfilling other conditions. Tracey's ex wants to place the responsibility for his relationship with their son on her shoulders, but that responsibility belongs to him.

9. Support Your Child

Talking to a child about mental illness, substance abuse, or domestic violence in his family isn't easy, but it is a necessary step toward helping him heal and thrive. With the support of a family counselor and other resources, you can help your child cope with the reality of his parent's personal struggles. The American Psychological Association's Magination Press offers books such as *Why Are You So Scared? A Child's Book about Parents with PTSD* for children who have witnessed violence or trauma or who have parents with mental illness (see the resources at the back of this book for more Magination Press titles as well as some helpful books for children about parental alcohol or other drug dependency).

Depending on the circumstances, allowing provisional (such as supervised) parenting time for a parent with a problem can serve to both honor the parent's rights and protect the children.

10. Get Immediate Help

If you believe you or your child to be in danger, seek immediate assistance from local law enforcement or call the National Domestic Violence hotline at 1-800-799-SAFE (7233) or TTY 1-800-787-3224.

11. Have a Plan B

With young children, if your ex is unreliable, you may choose to avoid telling them in advance that the other parent is coming for them, to minimize disappointment. However, for older children (and some younger ones), unexpected transitions from one parent to the other may be as difficult as, if not more difficult than, a disappointment. Consider which approach is more suitable for your child's disposition, and have a backup plan for the day (or evening), if need be.

Your child may feel frustrated, sad, angry, or disappointed if the other parent doesn't show up as scheduled. You can affirm those feelings and comfort your child without bashing the other parent. See chapter 5 for some suggestions to help you walk this fine line.

A Plan B also comes in handy if your ex is unwilling to be flexible with the schedule. "My husband Jeff and I always celebrated Christmas in July with the kids," says Marian, a mom of three and stepmom of two (all now adults). "His ex-wife insisted that because, in her opinion, Jeff never had true Christmas spirit, the boys should be with her every year. In the years that they were scheduled to be with us for Christmas, she would find a way to sabotage it. One year, she just flat out refused to bring them to us. It was awful.

"So the next year, instead of yet another trip to court—and funding our lawyer's Christmas—Jeff and I decided to get creative. Right after the Fourth of July, we started Christmas shopping. One Friday night, we hauled the decorations out of the basement and trimmed the tree. We played Christmas music and baked the whole weekend. The kids *loved* it. We turned what could have been an ongoing battle with his ex into years of wonderful memories."

A friend of Marian's thought that Jeff should have fought his ex in court to uphold the original agreement. "She said, 'But you let her win,'" Marian recalls. "I told her, 'No, she didn't win. The kids did.'"

12. Educate Yourself about Parental Alienation

While the idea of parental alienation as a "syndrome" is controversial, undeniably some co-parents manipulate their children in order to undermine their relationship with the other parent. If you are concerned that this is happening in your family, seek legal advice and consult resources such as the Center for Education on Parental

Alienation (kidsneedboth.org), the *Divorce Poison* book series by Dr. Richard A. Warshak, and Michael Jeffries's book *A Family's Heartbreak: A Parent's Introduction to Parental Alienation.*

13. Consider Parallel Parenting

If you and your co-parent remain entrenched in fighting, engage in highly dramatic and potentially dangerous behaviors with regard to each other, or are honestly afraid of each other, you may wish to consider *parallel parenting*. The concept of parallel parenting is adapted from sociologist Mildred Parten's observations in the 1930s of how very young children tend to play side by side (or parallel), using their own toys and leaving each other alone for the most part, before they learn to play together. Similarly, some co-parents are mired in such deep conflict that the best they are likely to be able to do is parent in a parallel fashion. While parallel parenting is not ideal for the children, some family court judges and parents themselves decide that this arrangement is preferable to constant exposure to nasty parental exchanges.

Whereas cooperative co-parenting is child-centered, parallel parenting is parent-focused. Here are some characteristics of parallel parenting:

+ Parents have little communication, except in cases of children's emergencies.

+ Parenting plans are rigid and highly detailed.

+ Instead of discussing or consulting with each other, parents *inform* each other about issues related to their children.

+ Transitions take place at a neutral or public location.

Parallel parenting minimizes parental interaction and reduces active conflict, but it can come at a very high cost to the children. Says Tracey of her and her ex's parallel parenting: "It clearly hurts our daughter, and I wish we could be done with this nonsense. We've been divorced for years, I have nothing to do with my ex's life, and he's not in mine. His hostility is…tiring, it's harmful, and I wish he would stop and think about what's best for our daughter. It seems to get worse every year, as she's old enough now to notice the tensions and ask him about them. He blames me, so then she comes back and asks me what it's all about, and I'm left trying to clear up the lie while spinning things as neutrally as possible and leaving her feeling like she's not a rope in a tug-of-war."

Tracey offers this advice to parents: "Unless a parent is violent or crazily intrusive, I really think [parallel parenting is] a selfish way of parenting. Go to therapy yourself, learn to deal with the other parent, deal with your own anger, fix your own life. It turns what should be a joy into a siege for the parents, and it leaves the children feeling split and miserable."

Tracey echoes the sentiments that Olivia, whose parents divorced when she was thirteen, shared with us:

> It was a hostile and unhealthy situation for me and my brother, and a very defining experience in my life. I am twenty-eight years old now, and my family's relationship turned into this parallel parenting format. I strongly believe that this isn't what is best for the children, but I do understand that sometimes adults cannot make it work, as hard as they try. After the divorce, my parents were emotionally drained and exhausted.
>
> As a teen, I was forced to protect my father and mother, [being careful] about what I say and how I say it, regarding the other. I was unable to share a whole half of myself with the other parent, which created distance between us. Even though it wasn't said, I could feel the anger between them, and it became something I had to tiptoe around [so] as not to hurt anyone's feelings. I became the adult, and they became the child. I began to resent my parents for their selfishness (as I saw it), because they couldn't get it together for us.

As an adult, this has truly affected who my brother and I became. Because I felt I was an adult at sixteen, I moved out. I graduated from high school without their help, worked a part-time job, and luckily I went to college and got a degree, on full scholarship. I hope to one day start a nonprofit working with families going through divorce. My brother wasn't so lucky. [Olivia didn't say anything more about her brother, so we can only guess what she meant by this: that the fallout from the divorce continues to negatively impact her brother's life.]

It would sound like this parallel parenting was a success for me, but I wouldn't say so. Even as an adult, I long to have parents that can communicate with each other. I long for memories of Christmases, birthdays, graduations, where all of my family could support me. I learned to hold all of my feelings inside, and this has translated itself into my own relationships. It still has affected my relationship with my parents, as I have learned that I can only depend on myself to get what I need from life. I trust very few people to do what is best for me, and this has created a façade of my personality, as very few people really get to know the real me.

You can read more reflections from adult children of divorce in the postscript to this book.

If you decide to parallel parent, we hope you will remain open to the possibility of more cooperative co-parenting in the future.

14. Consider Your Legal Options

If your ex persists in violating the parenting plan at the expense of your child's well-being, arguing about it has probably gotten you nowhere. Rather than remain in active conflict about it, document the details of the violations with dates, times, and other pertinent information, including your attempts to work with your ex and your ex's responses.

When a co-parent violates the plan, the other parent has the option of filing a motion asking a family court judge to hold the violating parent in contempt. But at that point, the plan is only as good as the measures the judge is willing to undertake to enforce it. A plan is just a tool and it has its limits. Its value comes from co-parents using it in the spirit in which it was created—hopefully a cooperative one.

Prior to filing a motion for contempt with the court, you may wish to send your ex a certified letter about the violations and request mediation at your shared expense. Consult a family law attorney in your area to find out what legal recourse you may have.

15. Don't Give Up ... Your Kids Are Worth It!

If co-parenting under difficult circumstances has you feeling discouraged and worried about the impact of parental conflict on your child, don't underestimate the power of your positive parental influence in the face of negativity. Focus on the power you *do* have to impact your child's life for the better, even though you may feel powerless when your child is not in your care.

We understand that it's hard to be the "bigger" co-parent. But hold on to the hope that your kids will "get it," in their own time. They will see that you've done the best you could as their parent, given the circumstances. Stay the course, because your character and your actions *do* matter...and because the children are always watching. The time, thoughts, patience, laughter, fun, and love that you share with your child means the world to her.

We would like to close this book with wishes for peace.

Peace to the parents who don't get a chance to laugh and have fun with their children because the other parent won't allow it.

Peace to the parents who feel as if they messed up at the outset of the divorce and want another chance with their children to do better.

Peace to the parents who are afraid that their children's love for the other parent somehow diminishes the children's love for them. (It doesn't.)

Peace to the children who live in two households and who simply want...peace.

Postscript

What Co-parents Can Learn from Adult Children of Divorce

Always put your own feelings toward your ex-partner on the back burner. Ask yourself: is this what I would do if I was parenting, as opposed to co-parenting?

—Carolyn Grona, founder of the blog *The Grown Up Child* (thegrownupchild.ca), a resource for adult children of divorce

As co-parents, we liken ourselves to scientists in a laboratory: seeking solutions to daily challenges, answering new questions, experimenting to see what works as we parent our children together to the best of our ability while living apart. By contrast, adults whose parents divorced when they were children are the living proof, the result of their parents' efforts. Even though every family is unique, co-parents still have much to learn from what adult children of divorce have told us about their experiences. Below are some reflections from this important perspective.

Feelings about their parents' decision to divorce:

"I'm sympathetic to that. If I had married the person I was dating at seventeen, I would most likely be divorced too. I have never felt any anger at my parents for their divorce."

On hearing the intimate details of the divorce and problems in the marriage:

"My father still has a lot of pain stemming from his divorce from my mother. So much so, that he has told me it sometimes interferes with his having a relationship with me. He has felt the need on a few occasions to tell me details surrounding the divorce. I can only assume he has done that in the hopes that I would relate to his pain. Unfortunately for him, it doesn't [work]. Over thirty years later, I still don't want to be involved in any of the gory details. I think for children of nuclear families it would be like hearing about your parents' sex life. It doesn't matter how old you get; you just don't want to know."

On what their parents and stepparents did well during times of transition, such as divorce, dating, and remarriage:

"My parents were very good about keeping me completely out of their divorce while I was young. I was never asked to choose between them or have any input on custody issues. I was never privy to their dating lives. I don't even remember meeting any of their significant others aside from my stepparents. In their remarriages, I was included as much as I could be. I was excited for both of my parents. I was happy to see them happy. In all these ways, my parents did a great job."

"My parents were careful with me regarding the divorce. They made sure to reiterate the fact that the divorce was not my fault and that I should never blame myself for it, and I really appreciate that. Also, my dad made a big effort to remain a part of my life. I saw him twice a month from the time of the divorce until I graduated high school and went to college. He also always paid child support and was very generous with it."

On what they wish the adults in their lives had done differently:

"I wish my parents had worked together more effectively overall, though I think they tried harder during times of transition [such as the divorce and subsequent remarriages]. They paid closer attention to what I would need. But during everyday life, their co-parenting skills weren't so strong. There was tension between them. I never felt really comfortable expressing the love I had for each of them with the other or with my stepparents, like it would be some kind of betrayal. The tension was palpable between my stepmother and mother. It always made me feel uncomfortable."

"I really wanted for my parents to be truly happy that I loved them both. That I could be excited to do something with one of them and feel comfortable enough to express that to the other. That I could be happy for each of them in their new lives and know in my heart that they were happy for each other as well. Because I felt like the 'secret keeper.' Like I couldn't just be myself and that I had to think about everything I would say. That I had to hide my feelings so that I wouldn't hurt theirs. And the more animosity I sensed between them, the more I felt like the obstacle to their happiness. That their lives would be easier had I never existed."

"My stepmother, Jane, treated me well at times, but also criticized me for a lot of things I did or who I was. She humiliated me in front of other people, and she pressured me to see her as a replacement for my mother. I don't recall my dad doing much to prevent this from happening, but recently I found a reference in an old journal that said my dad attempted to explain Jane's behavior to me. I'm sure that was meant to make me understand her better and make myself feel better that it wasn't my fault, but it didn't help me at all. They were married from the time I was eight [until I was] fifteen, a highly turbulent time which I would never wish on any child to take on the emotional problems of an adult, let alone someone only related by marriage. So my memories of my dad during this time are mostly of him standing ineffectually by, letting Jane treat me this way. I feel as though I was very vulnerable and unprotected, and caught between two households, trying to please everyone, which was impossible."

Words of advice for co-parents:

"I wish I had felt like my parents were parenting me together instead of parenting me only on 'their time.' When I was at Mom's, she was the parent and when I was at Dad's, he was. But weren't they both my parents, all of the time? That's what I struggled with and what I would hope co-parents would try to overcome."

"Co-parenting is difficult. Just [as with] parenting, there are no quick answers. No one-size-fits-all solutions. Every family and every child is different and therefore will require different things from you. It's a process. Something to strive toward. But never give up. Always do your best. Because there is no greater reward in this life than having a happy, comfortable, well-adjusted child to share in the rest of your days."

"Share time with the kids as much as possible. I think it's important to have both parents involved with the kids if at all possible. If you can, too, allow each other to be both the kids' disciplinarian and fun-time parent. I ended up having a really negative view of my mom because she was mostly the disciplinarian and my dad was my hero because all we did was have fun together."

"Try to be civil to one another when meetings must happen. My parents were pretty good about this when my dad would come to pick me up at my mom's house. They usually talked, even if begrudgingly at times, and that was good. It probably would've been much more upsetting to me if they had fought at these times, or conversely if they had not talked at all."

Words of advice for children in co-parenting families:

"Your parents' decision to divorce was about the fact that they no longer got along with each other, not about you. Trust me, neither of them is angry or mad at you. If you have a brother or sister, talk to them about the divorce. Share your feelings; rely on each other to talk to if you're not ready to talk to your parents. And when you are ready, talk to your parents about it too. They may be able to help you [better] understand why they divorced.... Sometimes you may feel sad about a divorce, sometimes you might feel happy. Your feelings will probably change over time, and that's okay. If you are feeling bad about it, please talk to someone you trust about your feelings—they can help you feel better. Try to [communicate as openly] with your family about divorce as you can. And if one of your parents remarries, try to be as accepting as you can toward their new spouse. But also remember that you have the right to express how you're thinking and feeling about the situation, so try not to be afraid to speak up if you're unhappy about something your new stepparent is doing."

"Be yourself. Express what you feel, not just what you think is expected. Don't lose yourself in an attempt to fit into your new surroundings. Acknowledge and explore your feelings, knowing that they are nothing to be ashamed of. Divorce *is* survivable. It hurts, but the pain fades. And there is a wealth of support available. Books, websites, talking to friends, and counseling are all things that have helped me significantly in the past. Writing is what helps me now. And please don't let either your parents' or your anger consume you. You love your parents. Both of them. And that's okay; not just okay, but the way it's supposed to be! Don't be scared of relationships. Don't set the bar so high that nobody will pass. Don't let the fear of making your parents' mistakes stop you from living your own life. Because your life is exactly that. Your own. So go live it."

On how their families' experiences with divorce and remarriage shaped them as adults:

"It has made me incredibly independent. A positive now, it comes from one of the negative results as a kid: feeling like the outsider or the strange one all the time. But as an adult, I've persevered through incredible trials. And I know I can stand on my own two feet. And I'll do anything to preserve and protect my family unit. That being said, I have also struggled. I suppressed almost all of my own feelings because I never felt comfortable expressing them. I never confided being hurt to my parents for fear of them feeling guilty. I never told them I was sad because I knew it would make them sad too. That's what so many of us children of divorce do. We feel the need to protect our parents instead of allowing them to protect us. We worry that if they knew the truth about our feelings they might break, so we hold it in. And [personally] I never really stopped [holding it in]. It became...my way of dealing with unpleasant things. I became really good at shutting down. So as an adult now, I'm focusing on...opening instead of closing."

On childhood memories that capture their feelings and experiences as children of divorce:

"I remember special times with my parents alone. I remember my mom trying to drive her Honda Civic out of a snow bank and me chanting with her: 'Come on, rear wheel drive. You can do it, rear wheel drive!' I remember my dad and me watching movies together—a favorite pastime of his—and I cherish that simple time I had alone with him. The bonds I have with my parents have been tested over the years. They are tested sometimes now. But I know those bonds run as deep as in any nuclear family. I know because I have a collection of memories just like these for each of them."

Resources

Books

After the Affair by Janis Abrahms Spring (with Michael Spring), HarperCollins Publishers, 1996

Contemplating Divorce: A Step-by-Step Guide to Deciding Whether to Saty or Go. by Susan Pease Gadoua, New Harbinger Publications, 2008

The D-Word: Divorce Through a Child's Eyes by Tara Eisenhard, iUniverse.com, 2012

Divorce Poison: Protecting the Parent-Child Bond from a Vindictive Ex by Richard A. Warshak, Harper Paperbacks, 2003

Divorce Poison: How to Protect Your Family from Bad-mouthing and Brainwashing by Richard A. Warshak, William Morrow Paperbacks, 2010

An Elephant in the Living Room: The Children's Book by Jill M. Hastings and Marion H. Typpo, Hazelden Foundation, 1994

A Family's Heartbreak: A Parent's Introduction to Parental Alienation by Michael Jeffries (with Joel Davies), A Family's Heartbreak, LLC 2009

For Teenagers Living with a Parent Who Abuses Alcohol/Drugs by Edith Lynn Hornik-Beer, iUniverse.com, 2001

Getting Divorced without Ruining Your Life: A Reasoned, Practical Guide to the Legal, Emotional and Financial Ins and Outs of Negotiating a Divorce Settlement by Sam Margulies, Simon & Schuster, 2001

The Good Karma Divorce: Avoid Litigation, Turn Negative Emotions into Positive Actions, and Get On with the Rest of Your Life by Michele Lowrance, Harper One, 2010

Helping Your Kids Cope with Divorce the Sandcastles Way by M. Gary Neuman (with Patricia Romanowski), Times Books, 1998

How to Heal a Broken Heart in 30 Days: A Day-by-Day Guide to Saying Good-bye and Getting On with Your Life by Howard Bronson and Mike Riley, Broadway Books, 2002

I Can Talk about What Hurts: A Book for Kids in Homes Where There's Chemical Dependency by Janet Sinberg and Dennis Daley, Hazelden, 1989

Let's Talk about It: Divorce by Fred Rogers and Jim Judkis, Puffin, 1998

My Dad Loves Me, My Dad Has a Disease: A Child's View: Living with Addiction by Claudia Black, Mac Publishing, 1997

The Smart Divorce: Proven Strategies and Valuable Advice from 100 Top Divorce Lawyers, Financial Advisers, Counselors, and Other Experts by Deborah Moskovitch, Chicago Review Press, 2007

Stepmonster: A New Look at Why Real Stepmothers Think, Feel, and Act the Way We Do by Wednesday Martin, Houghton Mifflin Harcourt, 2009

A Terrible Thing Happened: A Story for Children Who Have Witnessed Violence or Trauma by Margaret M. Holmes (illustrated by Cary Pillo), Magination Press, 2000

Why Are You So Sad? A Child's Book about Parental Depression by Beth Andrews (illustrated by Nicole Wong), Magination Press, 2002

Why Are You So Scared? A Child's Book about Parents with PTSD by Beth Andrews (illustrated by Katherine Kirkland), Magination Press, 2011

Websites

A Family's Heartbreak

afamilysheartbreak.com

Founded by a father, Michael Jeffries, this site provides information, advice, and support for parents who have suffered alienation from their children.

Bill of Rights for Children in Divorce and Dissolution Actions

afcc-nj.org/bill_of_rights.html

Here you will find the full text of the Bill of Rights for Children in Divorce and Dissolution Actions from chapter 1.

Café Smom

cafesmom.com

Created by Heather Hetchler, a co-parenting mom of four and a custodial stepmom of two, this site offers helpful tips and encouragement to "smoms" experiencing the challenges and joys of stepfamily life.

Center for Education on Parental Alienation

kidsneedboth.org

This site offers a variety of resources to help co-parents identify signs of and create strategies for dealing with parental alienation.

Co-Parenting 101

coparenting101.org

We created this blog to offer support, encouragement, and practical advice to those parenting across households after a divorce or breakup.

DivorceCare

www.divorcecare.org

Through this site, you can find a divorce recovery support group in your area, as well as books and CDs about divorce for adults and children.

DivorceNet.com

www.divorcenet.com

This site is a clearinghouse of information about divorce and family law, by state. You can also search for family law attorneys by zip code.

Family Court Services of the Third Judicial District of Idaho

www.familycourtservicesidaho.org/parenting

This site features multiple downloadable documents useful to co-parents writing a parenting plan.

Grit and Glory

gritandglory.com

Here Alece Ronzino, whose husband's infidelity led to the end of their marriage, blogs about starting life over.

Magination Press

www.apa.org/pubs/magination

The American Psychological Association's Magination Press publishes accessible self-help picture books, workbooks, and middle school and teen readers for kids and the adults who love and support them. The books address a wide range of psychological as well as everyday concerns such as bullying, mental and physical illness in families, parental substance abuse, self-esteem, and stepfamilies.

Parental Alienation Help

www.parentalalienationhelp.org

This site offers research, workbooks for parents, and other resources to increase awareness and understanding of parental alienation.

The Phoenix Ritual

www.newlifeafterdivorce.com/PDF/phoenixritual.pdf

The website New Life After Divorce makes available for free this series of recovery exercises.

Postcards from a Peaceful Divorce

www.postcardsfromapeacefuldivorce.com

Molly Monet is a co-parenting mom who hopes to inspire others by blogging about her postdivorce experiences, including her commitment to a peaceful parenting partnership.

Since My Divorce

www.sincemydivorce.com

Mandy Walker offers this blog as a forum for women to share stories of learning, growth, and rebuilding.

Single Dad

www.singledad.com

Richard "RJ" Jaramillo's site features an interactive social network, along with advice and referrals, for single dads.

Singlemommyhood

www.singlemommyhood.com

Despite the name, this is a resource for both single moms and single dads. Site founders Rachel Sarah and Dr. Leah Klungness welcome and answer questions from parents on a range of topics including dating, co-parenting, and money matters.

The Smart Divorce

thesmartdivorce.com

This is the website of Deborah Moskovitch, who provides private coaching and other resources for those looking to make smart decisions about divorce or about the next chapter in their lives.

This Cuckoo's Nest

www.thiscuckoosnest.com

A mom who shares a house with her ex-husband and her children blogs candidly here about "nesting" (see chapter 7).

US Customs and Border Protection INFO Center

help.cbp.gov/app/home

The US Customs and Border Protection website provides information about international travel with children and the process for obtaining a passport for a child.

When the Flames Go Up

whentheflamesgoup.com

This is a shared blog written by co-parents Doug French and Magda Pesceyne, who are divorced from each other. The blog offers a close look into their parenting partnership.

Other Resources

National Domestic Violence hotline: 1-800-799-SAFE (7233) or TTY 1-800-787-3224

References

Abel, K. N.d. "Dating after Divorce: What It Means for Kids." FamilyEducation.com. http://life.familyeducation.com/divorce/dating/29599.html.

American Bar Association (ABA) Center for Professional Responsibility. 2010. "Rule 1.7: Conflict of Interest: Current Clients." http://www.americanbar.org/groups/professional_responsibility/publications/model_rules_of_professional_conduct/rule_1_7_conflict_of_interest_current_clients.html.

Aslanian, S. 2012. "Never-Married Parents Get Help from Special Court." NPR.org, May 7. http://www.npr.org/2012/05/07/152157287/never-married-parents-get-help-from-special-court.

Bamberger, J. C. 2009. "Moms Inspired to Change History." MSN Living, n.d. http://living.msn.com/family-parenting/moms-inspired-to-change-history-3.

Bauserman, R. 2002. "Child Adjustment in Joint-Custody versus Sole-Custody Arrangements: A Meta-Analytic Review." *Journal of Family Psychology* 16: 91–102.

Center for Parental Responsibility. 2004. "The Need for Reform in Minnesota's Child Custody Statutes and Awards." http://cpr-mn.org/Documents/Legislative%20Packet%20Part%201.doc.

David, L., and K. Uhrenholdt. 2010. *The Family Dinner: Great Ways to Connect with Your Kids, One Meal at a Time*. New York: Grand Central Life & Style. Excerpted as "My Family Dinner After Divorce," *The Huffington Post*. November 9. http://www.huffingtonpost.com/laurie-david/my-family-dinner-after-di_b_779277.html.

DeVaris, J., S. Forlenza, D. Franklin, S. Saul, P. Sobel, and F. Weiss. N.d. "Bill of Rights for Children in Divorce and Dissolution Actions." Adapted from "The Children's Bill of Rights" developed by the American Bar Association's Family Law Section, and modified and expanded by the New Jersey Chapter of the Association of Family and Conciliation Courts' Special Projects Committee. http://afcc-nj.org/bill_of_rights.html.

Gilman, P. 2012. "My Good Divorce: How One Woman Found Happiness Separating." *The Daily Beast*. June 9. http://www.thedailybeast.com/articles/2012/06/09/my-good-divorce-how-one-woman-found-happiness-separating.html.

Grona, C. 2009. "Divorce Doesn't Hurt? Actually...It Does." *The Grown Up Child* (blog), November 20. http://thegrownupchild.ca/2009/11/divorce-hurts/.

Jeffries, M. 2008. *A Family's Heartbreak: A Parent's Introduction to Parental Alienation*. With J. Davies. Stamford, CT: A Family's Heartbreak, LLC.

Joakimidis, Y. 1994. "Back to the Best Interests of the Child: Towards a Rebuttable Presumption of Joint Residence, 2nd edition." Policy monograph from the Joint Parenting Association, Adelaide, South Australia. http://cpr-mn.org/Documents/Back%20to%20the%20Best%20Interests.pdf.

Kübler-Ross, E. 1969. *On Death and Dying*. New York: Macmillan.

Kübler-Ross, E., and D. Kessler. 2005. *On Grief and Grieving: Finding the Meaning of Grief through the Five Stages of Loss*. New York: Scribner.

Kuhn, R., and J. Guidubaldi. 1997. "Child Custody Policies and Divorce Rates in the US." Paper presented at the 11th Annual Conference of the Children's Rights Council, Washington, DC, October 23–26. http://deltabravo.net/cms/plugins/content/content.php?content.288.

Martin, W. 2009. *Stepmonster: A New Look at Why Real Stepmothers Think, Feel, and Act the Way We Do.* Boston: Houghton Mifflin Harcourt.

McKenna, S. N.d. "Healing Hurting Hearts: Healing Your Child's Heart during Divorce." *Divorce Support* (blog). http://divorcesupport.about.com/od/meetingyourchildsneeds/a/healinghearts.htm.

Moskovitch, D. 2007. *The Smart Divorce: Proven Strategies and Valuable Advice from 100 Top Divorce Lawyers, Financial Advisers, Counselors, and Other Experts.* Chicago: Chicago Review Press.

Neil, M. 2007. "Kinder, Gentler Collaborative Divorce Also Costs Less." *ABA Journal* (online), December 18. http://www.abajournal.com/news/article/kinder_gentler_collaborative_divorce_also_costs_less/.

Nelson, L. 1995. "Ten Commandments of Co-Parenting." *Minnesota Parent*, May.

Neuman, M. G. 1998. *Helping Your Kids Cope with Divorce the Sandcastles Way.* With P. Romanowski. New York: Times Books.

Philyaw, D., and M. D. Thomas. *Co-Parenting 101* (blog). 2008–2012. http://coparenting101.org.

———. 2009. "The Truth about NonCustodial Parents: An Interview with Rebekah Spicuglia." *Co-Parenting 101* (blog), July 9.http://coparenting101.org/2009/07/the-truth-about-noncustodial-parents-an-interview-with-rebekah-spicuglia/.

———. 2012. "Bird's Nest Co-Parenting 101." *Co-Parenting 101* (blog), February 20. http://coparenting101.org/2012/02/birds-nest-co-parenting-101/.

Philyaw, D., M. Thomas, and T. Mbonisi. 2011. "Celebrating Stepdads" (includes an interview with R. Deal). *CoParenting Matters* (online radio program), April 10. http://www.blogtalk radio.com/coparentingmatters/2011/04/11/ co-parenting-matters.

Ronzino, A. 2010. Tweet, December 3. http://twitoaster.com/ gritandglory/the-only-thing-harder-on-your-heart-than-forgiveness-is-unforgiveess-choose-to-forgive-today-again/.

Rose, I. 2009. *The Package Deal: My (Not-So) Glamorous Transition from Single Gal to Instant Mom.* New York: Three Rivers Press.

Shackelton, E. 2006. "Co-Parenting after Divorce." Colorado State University Extension newsletter. October. Fort Collins, CO. http://www.ext.colostate.edu/pubs/COLUMNCC/cc061009. html.

US Bureau of the Census, Housing and Household Economic Statistics Division. 2011. Current Population Reports, Series P60-240, *Custodial Mothers and Fathers and Their Child Support: 2009.* Washington, DC: US Government Printing Office. http:// www.census.gov/prod/2011pubs/p60-240.pdf.

Deesha Philyaw is a freelance writer whose work has appeared in *Essence* and *Bitch* magazines, as well as the *Washington Post*. Her writing has been anthologized in several collections including *Literary Mama: Reading for the Maternally Inclined*; *When We Were Free to Be: Looking Back at a Children's Classic and the Difference It Made*; and *The Cassoulet Saved Our Marriage: True Tales of Food, Family, and How We Learn to Eat*. She is the co-founder of coparenting101.org

Michael D. Thomas works in the financial services industry and is the co-founder of coparenting101.org.

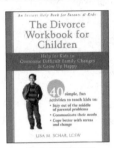

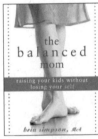